GLACIER MOUNTAINEERING

An Illustrated Guide to Glacier Travel and Crevasse Rescue

Andy Tyson & Mike Clelland !

FALCONGUIDES ®

GUILFORD, CONNECTICUT
HELENA, MONTANA

AN IMPRINT OF THE GLOBE PEQUOT PRESS

Thank you!

Mike and I would like to express thanks to all who have helped in this project.

The words, techniques, and systems that are represented in this book are not original. They are a synthesis developed over years of climbing and educating. Many individuals had a role in both supporting the process as well as directly contributing. Indirect influences are easily as important as direct contributions. Thank you to Molly Loomis, David and Henrietta Tyson, Tony Jewel, Don Sharaf, Chas Day, Chris Sanok, Gary Wilmot, Scot Kane, Michelle Escudero, Tim Hopkin, Rachael Knapp, Colby Coombs, Vern Tejas, Willi Prittie, Neil McCarthy, Mark Johnson, Rick Klebanow, Tom Liddle, Monica Miller, Ravi Kumar, Krishnan Kutty, Tashi guest house in Hampi, Michael Kennedy, Phil Powers, Kevin Mahoney, Andy Wise, Mike Wood, Meg Perdue, Joe Richert, Pete and Molly Absolon, Tom Bole, George Newbury, Willy Peabody, Harold Vanderpool, John Hauf, John Irish, Joe Austin, Eric Sawyer, Jim Ferguson, Natalie Kaplan, Brad Sawtell, Matt Scullion, Aileen Brew, Lynne Wolf, Miss White, Mark Jordan, Don Ford, Blaine Smith, Darrell Miller, Duane Raleigh, Angela Patnode, Brien Sheedy, Dave McGivern, Allen O'Bannon, Shawn Benjamin, Liz Rumzey, Peter Agliata, Hunter Dahlgerg, Marco Johnson, and more!

— *Andy & Mike*

To buy books in quantity for corporate use
or incentives, call **(800) 962–0973**
or e-mail **premiums@GlobePequot.com**.

FALCONGUIDES®

Library of Congress Cataloging-in-Publication Data is available on file.
ISBN 978-0-7627-4862-4

Printed in the United States of America
10 9 8 7 6 5 4 3 2 1

Warning: Climbing is a dangerous sport. You can be seriously injured or die.
Read the following before you use this book.

This is an instruction book about climbing, a sport that is inherently dangerous. Do not depend solely on information from this book for your personal safety. Your mountaineering safety depends on your own judgment based on competent instruction, experience, and a realistic assessment of your climbing ability.

There are no warranties, either expressed or implied, that this instruction book contains accurate and reliable information. There are no warranties as to fitness for a particular purpose or that this book is merchantable. Your use of this book indicates your assumption of the risk of death or serious injury as a result of climbing's risks and is an acknowledgment of your own sole responsibility for your safety in climbing or in training for climbing. The Globe Pequot Press and the authors assume no liability for accidents happening to, or injuries sustained by, readers who engage in the activities described in this book.

Contents

Abandon all hope without three on rope, ye who enter here.
— *old glacier-travel saying*

You'd better know what you're doing...
and do it NOW!

The four of us, Tom, Mark, Rachael, and I, were moving camp across an unnamed glacier to try another peak after a successful new route on Mount Bear in the Wrangell-Saint Elias range of eastern Alaska. For the past two weeks we had been traveling as one rope of four people. This day, however, we decided to go as two teams of two. Splitting the rope let us more easily rotate leading through the chaotic glacier, but only left one person on each rope to catch a fall into a crevasse.

I was route finding through a zone of jumbled ice blocks and crevasses caused by two converging glaciers. We were about halfway across the quarter-mile glacier. I was wanding the route for our return, putting a marker in every time Tom got to the last one and yelled "wand." The snow surface was wind crusted in some spots and powdery in others. We were wearing snowshoes and had full mountaineering packs. I had a wand in one hand and an ice axe in the other. My rope mate, Mark, knew it was a weird area, and was alert and ready to jump into self-arrest mode.

It's preferable to master these skills someplace other than an icy crevasse!

The crust under me collapsed and I dropped about three inches. Suddenly, with a WHOMP, a four- by 10-foot hole opened around me, and I fell another 30 feet, the rope knifing through the snowpack back to Mark, who was also standing above the same crevasse. My fall ended as abruptly as it began, and I was relieved to see that the crevasse under Mark was more thickly covered with snow.

I worried that someone else might fall in if they approached the crevasse to check on me. I was faced with two options. I could prusik up the rope, an unsavory move because further weighting the rope would cause it to cheese wire over to Mark, possibly pulling him in. Or, I could stem and climb up the crevasse walls, which were about as far apart as a doorway.

I pulled off my pack, took off my snowshoes, put on my crampons, and pulled out my second ice tool. Moving my prusiks up the rope as a self-belay, I climbed and stemmed 20 feet to a ledge, where I hand hauled my pack. I then climbed high enough to pop my head out of the crevasse and yell that all was fine.

Rachael, from the other team, crawled toward me, placed a snow picket, and belayed me for the final few feet.

Though the situation was scary, we were prepared, each of us well schooled in glacier travel and crevasse rescue. Many such incidents more benign than this one don't end so happily. Every year mountaineers and glacier hikers are badly injured or killed in crevasse falls. Some are prepared and their accidents are the result of bad luck, but many others prefer to roll the dice, thinking they are immune to the many hazards a glacier presents.

Know this: The unprepared might squeak by once or twice, but eventually almost everyone who crosses a glacier falls in a crevasse. My fall was a mere delay. How is yours going to end?

The following book is about how to safely cross glaciers and how to extract yourself from crevasses. Everything in the book is meant to be practiced. These are skills that you can only learn by doing. Practice them in a safe, controlled environment, such as your lawn, in a tree, or on an unglaciated snowfield. As you practice you'll discover a myriad of other useful tidbits on your own. Until you get out and go through the ropes, you haven't learned anything.

This book is not a comprehensive mountaineering manual. We assume that you are already familiar with many outdoor skills, including fundamental rope work, avalanche safety, and first aid. If you lack any of these skills, learn them from a credible instructor before delving into the labyrinth of glacier travel and crevasse rescue.

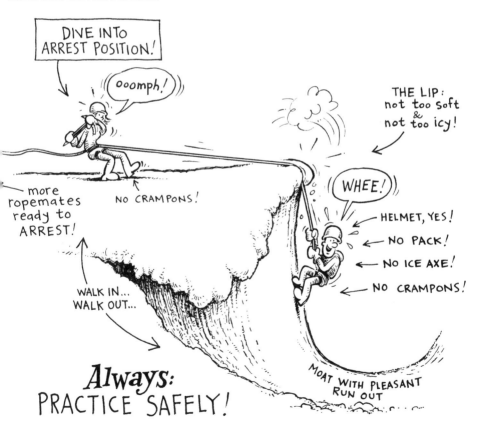

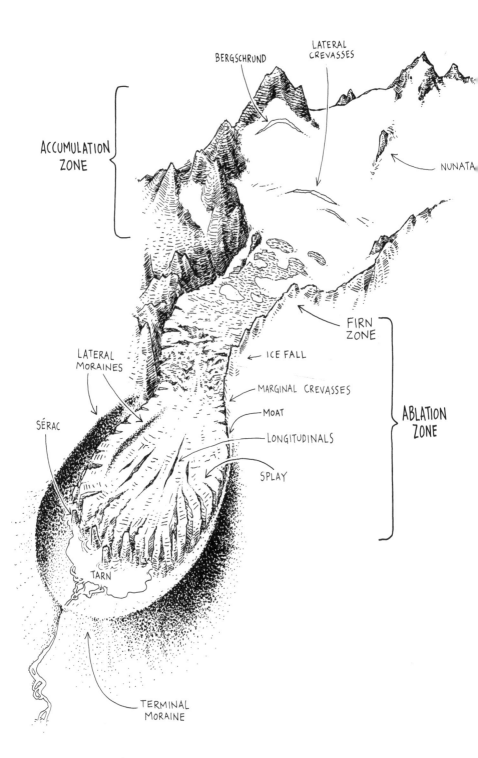

ACCUMULATION ZONE

BERGSCHRUND

LATERAL CREVASSES

NUNATA

FIRN ZONE

LATERAL MORAINES

ICE FALL

MARGINAL CREVASSES

MOAT

LONGITUDINALS

ABLATION ZONE

SÉRAC

SPLAY

TARN

TERMINAL MORAINE

A glacier is like a river of ice, constantly moving, molding to and sculpting the terrain it crosses. Glaciers form when snow builds up in the mountains where it is too cold to melt. This build-up can take thousands of years. As the snow accumulates the underlying layers metamorphose into ice. When the ice gets 80 to 100 feet thick its tremendous weight causes it to "flow." Gravity has its say, requiring the ice to flow down hill, following slopes and valleys. The two defining attributes of a glacier, then, are dense ice and flow due to gravity.

Glaciers vary in size: some may be as small as a football field while others can be miles across and hundreds of miles long. Greenland and Antarctica are examples of icecaps, landmasses almost entirely covered in glacial ice. Glaciers can also be relatively thin, say 100 feet, while others can be many thousands of feet thick. Understanding the guts of any glacier is critical to avoiding its dangers.

Ablation and accumulation zones

In the glacier's accumulation zone more snow falls than melts. Think of the accumulation zone as the glacial headwaters.

Below the accumulation zone you have the ablation, or wasting zone, where more snow melts than falls. The firn line, or more accurately firn zone, is the boundary between the accumulation and ablation zones. The elevation of the firn zone changes from year to year, depending on snowfall and temperatures. Banner snow years combined with cool summers, for example, cause the accumulation zone to get bigger and the firn zone to drop. Likewise, dry winters and warm summers cause the firn zone to retreat up glacier.

Below The Firn Zone

This is a strange world of wind- and sun-carved ice, bright and hard, slippery with lots of water, dirt, and rock. Below the firn line a glacier is generally bare ice and rock, with patches of snow or névé (old, dense snow). Snow is the stuff that fell that year. Névé is the stuff that fell in previous years that is still around but hasn't turned to ice yet. Névé is harder and more stable than snow, but not much.

Below Firn Line

Travel below the firn line isn't inherently tricky, because crevasses and other hazards are usually easy to see and sidestep. Most of the time you'll travel unroped on the "dry" glacier.

Snow below the firn zone, however, should be avoided. Above firn you are roped and traveling together, ready to deal with an unexpected crevasse fall. Below firn you're unroped and therefore unprepared to deal with the unexpected surprises that might be hiding under patches of snow. I've seen frighteningly large holes under innocuous-looking patches of snow. Snow below firn is usually thin and sticks around in cold places like spots covering deep crevasses or old moulins. Walk only on the bare ice. Never step on snow without either probing it for hidden dangers, or roping up, anchoring, and belaying one another across the hazard.

A common mistake is to rope up and move together across the bare ice, thinking that you'll be able to self-arrest and catch your partner should he fall in a crevasse. In reality, self-arresting on ice is nearly impossible, and the rope serves only to drag the entire team into the crevasse. If you are on bare ice and need extra security, stop, anchor, and belay. Common times to rope up and belay in the ablation zone include any time the ice is blanketed by a recent snowfall, when you must cross a sketchy crevasse, and when you must ascend or descend steep ice or rock slopes.

As you near the firn zone you'll gradually encounter more snow. Here you'll have to decide when to break out the rope. When the glacier is mostly covered in snow or névé — good mediums for self-arresting — it is probably safe to rope up and move together. If in doubt about the hazards near the firn zone, rope up.

Crevasses

Snowfall and air temperature are the glacier's budget. Balancing this budget is much less dynamic than, say, a flash flood, since a glacier is slower to react to climactic changes. Nonetheless, a glacier does act, and with dramatic results.

Like a river, a glacier can be choppy on the surface and relatively calm underneath. Crevasses are a glacier's waves, and can go down 150 to 200 feet. Below that depth, the weight of the overlying ice causes the deeper ice to ooze into a solid, unbroken mass, like silly putty.

You can guess or see where most crevasses are on a glacier. Just as a river's surface churns where the water flows over drops, rocks, or other obstacles, a glacier's surface tends to fracture in predictable patterns at drops, in narrow channels, on the outside edge of large bends, over icefalls, and at the snout as the glacier widens into a valley. The surface of the glacier is under stress in these areas, so they are called zones of tension.

Convexities are places where the glacier is pulling apart and the surface is under tension — expect crevasses here. Concavities are places where the

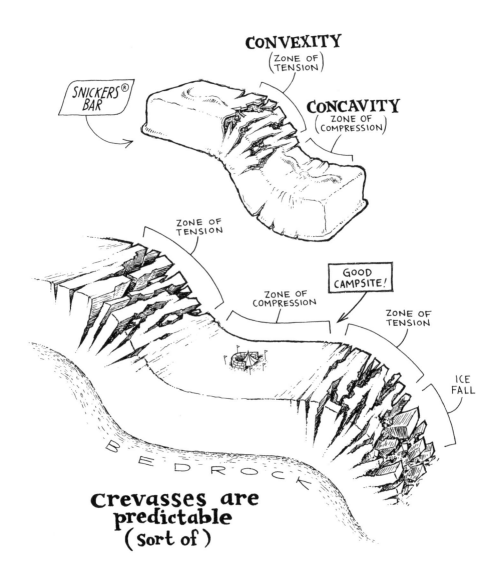

CONVEXITY
(ZONE OF
TENSION)

SNICKERS®
BAR

CONCAVITY
(ZONE OF
COMPRESSION)

ZONE OF
TENSION

GOOD
CAMPSITE!

ZONE OF
COMPRESSION

ZONE OF
TENSION

ICE
FALL

BEDROCK

Crevasses are predictable (Sort of)

surface is under compression — crevasses aren't likely here. Often, the glacier has a series of convexities and concavities so there is a series of crevasse fields and icefalls with less-crevassed terrain in between. Both occur due to differences in the bedrock the ice flows over and the curving channel it follows. Your safest route will be a careful linking of minimally crevassed concavities.

To find these good travel zones, study your map, scramble to a high vantage point, and examine the glacier, or get a glimpse during a flyover in an airplane.

The above are only general guidelines — glaciers are unpredictable. Crevasses can develop anywhere the glacier flows over an unseen and unpredictable object, such as a boulder, hump, or hole. Always be prepared for the unexpected, no matter how benign the glacier's surface appears.

Snow bridges

During the winter, snow builds up on either side of a crevasse. Slowly, snow may bridge the gap between the crevasse sides. Snow bridges are thin and weak at birth, but with enough snow and time can become thick and strong.

At lower elevations and latitudes the temperature warms up in the spring. The daytime sun and air temperature melt the upper part of the snowpack, allowing water to percolate through the rest of it. Then it refreezes overnight. This process, called the melt-freeze cycle, strengthens the snowpack, causing it to become super dense and hard. Sometimes bridges can be surprisingly strong in the melt-freeze snowpack.

At higher elevations and colder latitudes this melt-freeze cycle might never happen. Here, the snowpack does not consolidate and generally stays soft and weak throughout the year. Bridges in soft, cold snowpack areas may be thick but quite weak.

Snow bridges are what crevassed glacier travel is all about. Running into one doesn't mean you should run away. A snow bridge, even a sagging one, can be solid, especially if you are traveling early in the morning after a hard freeze. Evaluate the conditions to decide if you should cross the bridge or find an alternate route around it. To test the bridge, bang on it with a shovel, whap it with your ice axe, kick it with your snowshoe (don't fall in!). If you are just getting familiar with the conditions in the area, bash away the snow cover to see what's underneath.

Most snow bridges will be thinner in the middle or on the uphill edge, which is no problem provided the entire bridge is strong enough to support

LATE SUMMER
(Bare ice)

FALL
(first snow)

EARLY WINTER
(cracks begin to get covered)

MID WINTER
(Huge snow pack, everything is covered)

SPRING
(Melting season begins)

MID SUMMER
(bridges barely holding)

SOFT COLD SNOWPACK

examples:
- Alaska range
- Himalaya

un-cohesive frost crystals

- DRY SNOW
- COLD WINTERS
- HI-ALTITUDE
- WEAKLY BONDED SNOW

incredible X-RAY CROSS SECTIONS

MELT-FREEZE SNOWPACK

examples:
- Cascades
- Patagonia
- Canadian Coastal Range

POTENTIALLY PRETTY SOLID

- WET, HEAVY SNOW
- WARM WINTERS
- LOWER ALTITUDES
- WELL BONDED SNOW

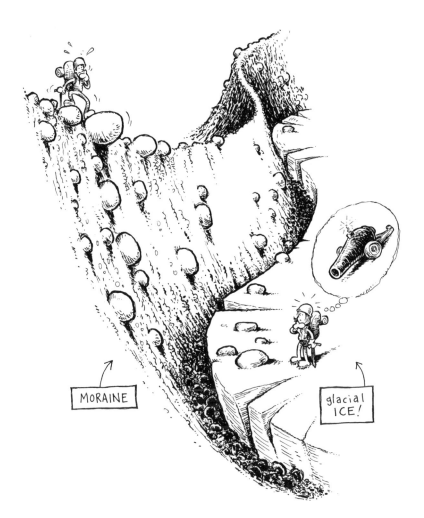

MORAINE

glacial
ICE!

you. Probe in front of you to find thin or weak spots as you cross. If you find a weak spot, use the probe to evaluate the other side and see if you can just step across the weak spot. If crossing the bridge seems prudent but you aren't 100-percent sure the bridge will hold, consider crawling or putting on skis or snowshoes to better distribute your weight. Have your (anchored) partner belay you across if things are really sketchy. Communicate with your team, and mark the perceived obstacle with wands if you intend to descend by the same route.

When you cross a series of bridges, learn as you go — if the previous bridge held and the next one you encounter is similar ... try it! Agonizing over each similar bridge can add a good bit of stress and time to your travel.

Moraines

A glacier acts like a giant bulldozer, pushing rocks and debris on its journey down valley. When the glacier recedes, it leaves its cargo of rocks and dirt in hills along its margins (flanks) and at its toe. These landforms are called moraines, and are composed of unsorted rocky material. These steep-sloped hills are probably the most geologically unstable rock piles on earth, and, because they are constantly eroding, pose serious objective hazards.

Long debris hills that run with the glacier (parallel to its edges) are called lateral moraines. A hill or rise stretching across the valley at the end or toe of the glacier is a terminal or end moraine. When two glaciers come together, their lateral moraines join to form a medial moraine.

A medial moraine can be your friend. Compression due to the glaciers meeting and the differential melting due to the rocks in the ice, help to make them good, rocky travel zones. This doesn't always hold true, but is usually worth a try. On large glaciers you may encounter numerous medial moraines, and on small glaciers there may be none. Medial moraines are also choice campsites when you are below the firn zone.

To see where the hazards really are, you might need to bash open some cracks!

Surface rivers and moulins

Below the firn line the glacial surface is alive with water from melting ice. In unbroken or non-crevassed areas this surface melt forms streams and rivers. Watercourses are a good sign: if water can flow across the surface of the ice, crevasses aren't likely nearby. These streams and rivers can, however, be challenging to cross. The water is racing fast in super-smooth channels, and water levels can rise and fall rapidly. Watch out!

To cross a pesky watercourse, wait until early morning after a cold night, when the water is likely low, and consider wearing crampons. Or, you might be able to hike upstream, find a place where the waterflow branches into

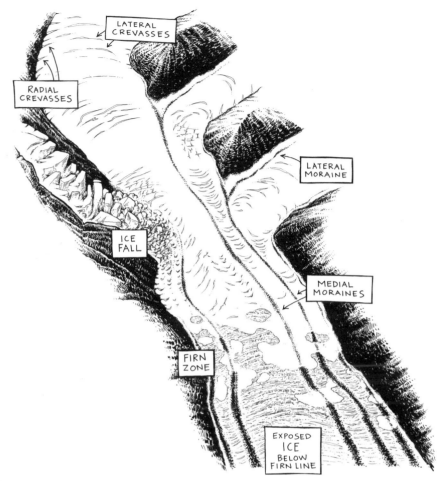

LATERAL CREVASSES

RADIAL CREVASSES

LATERAL MORAINE

ICE FALL

MEDIAL MORAINES

FIRN ZONE

EXPOSED ICE BELOW FIRN LINE

smaller, more manageable streams, and cross there. Checking downstream may also be an option, where you may encounter a moulin, or giant drain hole, where the water channels under the glacier. Though these holes allow easy passage around the stream, steer well clear of the moulin death trap.

Seracs and icefalls

When a glacier spills over a large cliff it breaks up, causing unstable icefalls and blocks, or seracs. These are some of mountaineering's greatest hazards. Since both are driven by gravity, they can collapse at any moment regardless of weather or temperature.

Icefalls and seracs kill novice and expert mountaineers alike. Your best defense is to avoid them. When that isn't possible, minimize your exposure by moving quickly through the danger zone, which isn't always apparent. For instance, that serac 4000 feet overhead may not seem like much of a menace, but it could calve off a block that could land on the snowslope under it, triggering a massive avalanche that sweeps the entire glacier. Also, icefalls and seracs aren't always visible — they can be tucked out of sight.

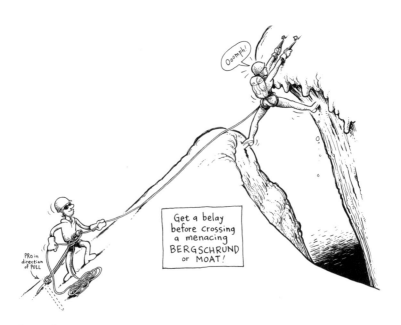

Bergschrunds

At the head of the glacier you have a large crevasse called the bergschrund. Technically the bergschrund isn't a crevasse; rather it's a crack between the snowfield high on the mountain and the glacial ice. The bergschrund is important because it is always there and presents a formidable obstacle, one that doesn't follow the 200-foot-deep maximum of crevasses — bergschrunds can seemingly plunge to the bowels of the earth. On the positive side, bergschrunds are typically high in the accumulation zone, and filled or partly filled with snow. Crossing one can be as simple as stepping over or wading across (belayed, of course). In extreme instances where the "schrund" isn't filled in you might rappel or lower into the crack and climb up the opposite side.

Moats

As the name suggests, a moat is a deep trench that forms along the edge of a snow field, where it melts against the warmer rock, dirt, or grass. Sometimes it is necessary to treat a moat like a bergschrund (rope up and belay across). In all situations, keep a careful watch for ice- and rock fall.

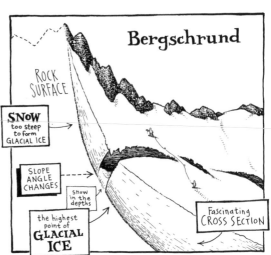

HUMPING the MONSTER LOAD
on a glacier makes travel
very dangerous and self rescue
potentially impossible!

What if I fall in?

M ike and I work 30-day mountaineering expeditions where we head out into the wilderness with a bunch of novices and lots of gear. We prefer the simple, streamlined approach to glacier travel, taking only what's needed and leaving all the fancy stuff in the store. This doesn't mean we skimp on safety, we just try to do more with less. For a gear reality check, read about early mountaineering expeditions on massive mountains. They did it with less.

What follows is the gear you can't do without. You'll notice that most of it is specific to glacier travel. This is because we assume that anyone setting foot on a glacier already has the basic skills and equipment necessary for snow and ice camping. We also assume that you are adept at basic mountaineering. If you lack knowledge in either department, read this book, then back up and learn some more.

Also in this chapter, beginning on page 22, you'll find all the knots you need for basic glacier travel and rope work.

Harness

A simple, lightweight, adjustable harness is all you need for glacier travel, where you constantly fiddle with your clothing layers. An unpadded harness is fine — your clothing will act as padding and it fits more neatly under a pack's waist belt than a bulky, padded harness. Adjustable leg loops accommodate a variety of layers, and an easily added "butt -floss clip" allows the leg loops to be dropped without untying from the rope when nature calls.

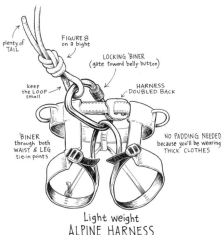

plenty of TAIL

FIGURE 8 on a bight

LOCKING 'BINER (gate toward belly-button)

HARNESS DOUBLED BACK

keep the LOOP small

'BINER through both WAIST & LEG tie-in points

NO PADDING NEEDED because you'll be wearing THICK CLOTHES

Light weight
ALPINE HARNESS

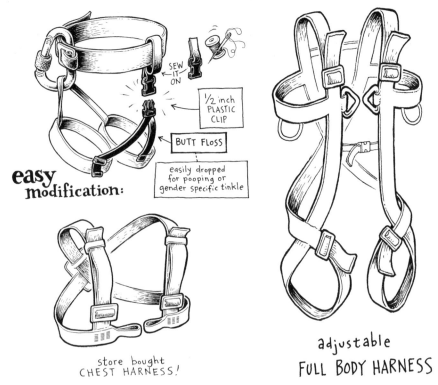

easy
modification:

SEW
IT
ON

½ inch
PLASTIC
CLIP

BUTT FLOSS

easily dropped
for pooping or
gender specific tinkle

store bought
CHEST HARNESS!

adjustable
FULL BODY HARNESS

If you are purchasing a harness just for glacier travel, consider a full-body harness. These look unwieldy, but are the most comfortable with a pack on, and, because there's only one attachment point, simplify clipping to the rope over a sit/chest-harness combination.

Chest and full-body harnesses

A crevasse fall with a big pack will flip you upside down unless you wear a chest harness or full-body harness to keep you upright. Flipping is dangerous and painful. A super-light summit pack probably won't flip you over, so you can skip the chest harness when you're traveling light.

The chest harness has one drawback: when you drop into self-arrest mode to catch your partner, the chest harness squeezes your torso toward your waist, which is painful for the five to 10 minutes it takes to build an anchor and un-weight the harness. Use a full-body harness and you'll avoid the squeeze scenario altogether.

You can buy any number of good chest harnesses, but you can also make your own. An easy way to make one is to tie an eight-foot piece of webbing in a loop with a water knot (page 22), and cross this over your shoulders. A saggy and loose chest harness doesn't cut it. In order to do its job it needs to be pretty snug — and this can be uncomfortable.

Another solution is to use a clip-in point on your backpack shoulder strap. To be effective this must be strong and still allow you to get out of your backpack in an emergency.

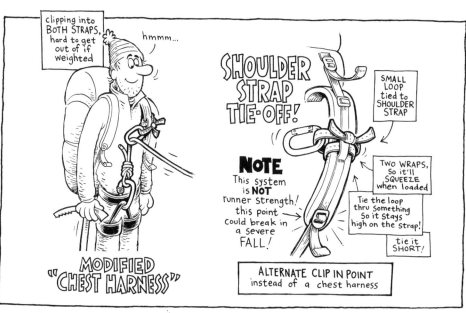

Crampons

Crampons are a necessity. A good pair will be easy to get on and off your boots. "Step-in" type bindings are the fastest to operate and secure, but only work on boots with dedicated grooves in the heel and toe. The new hybrid bindings use a plastic or nylon toe strap and a heel lever or heel strap. This design works on more types of boots than does the standard step-in.

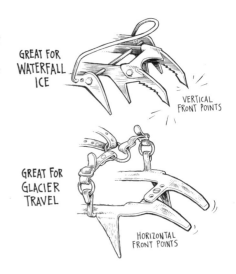

GREAT FOR WATERFALL ICE

VERTICAL FRONT POINTS

GREAT FOR GLACIER TRAVEL

HORIZONTAL FRONT POINTS

Avoid rigid frames with vertically oriented side rails and front points meant for waterfall ice climbing. These are heavy and make walking awkward; they act as cookie cutters, clogging with soft snow.

Sometimes you end up with your crampons on in wet snow, and they "ball up" with snow. Usually this is a good sign to take them off. When the terrain requires that you keep your crampons on in these conditions, bang them with your ice-axe shaft every few steps to clear out the snow.

Tip: When the surface ice is rough enough to walk on without crampons, take them off. Walking in crampons is hard on your ankles and knees. If you do encounter a short stretch of smooth ice, use your ice axe to chop a couple of steps.

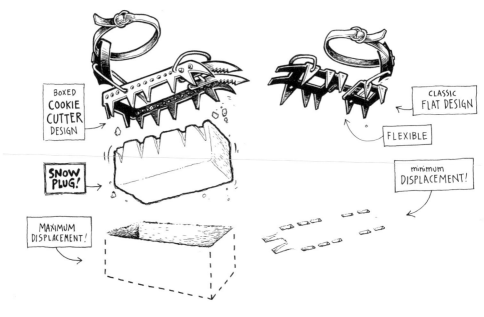

BOXED COOKIE CUTTER DESIGN

CLASSIC FLAT DESIGN

FLEXIBLE

SNOW PLUG!

minimum DISPLACEMENT!

MAXIMUM DISPLACEMENT!

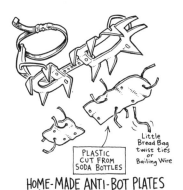

HOME-MADE ANTI-BOT PLATES
(these should last a whole trip)

PLASTIC CUT FROM SODA BOTTLES

Little Bread Bag twist ties or Bailing Wire

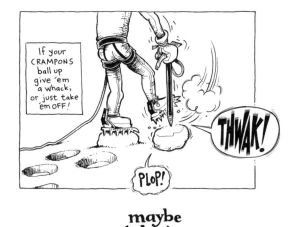

If your CRAMPONS ball up give 'em a whack, or just take 'em OFF!

THWAK!

PLOP!

maybe take 'em off?

Hmmmm...

BOOTS DESIGNED FOR SNOW TRAVEL

CRAMPONS DESIGNED FOR ICE TRAVEL

Yeti tracks?

SNOW

Anti-balling (anti-bot) plates can be added to crampon bottoms to help shed snow. These work pretty well but are not a necessity (read: extra weight!). Crafty folks can make their own out of plastic (like cut-up kiddie sleds). Custom cut and then wire them to the bottom of your crampons (Note that these are not super durable — they will usually last for a trip.

remove the FOAM INSOLES from overboots before wearing CRAMPONS

fit the toe & heel bail perfectly!

this may involve RE-ADJUSTING the crampons

DON'T TRIP YOURSELF!

GAAK!

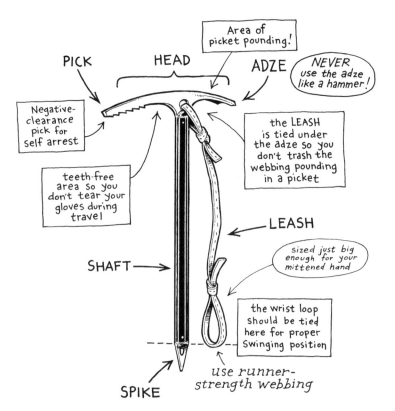

Ice axe

This is your main tool. You use it for everything from arresting falls to setting up camp. There are radical, super-techno vertical-ice tool designs, but for glaciers, your basic "piolet" with a classic-curve pick is ideal. A piolet's pick design gives you good self-arrest control; the adze works well for chopping away rotten surface ice; the straight shaft plunges easily into hard snow; and the tooth- and bolt-free head comfortably fits your hand. Avoid some of the super-light axes, which can bend or break.

To prevent your axe from getting lost when you fall in a crevasse, you'll need to attach it to you via a leash or tether. A standard wrist leash tied through the eye of the ice-axe head is the simplest, but a tether makes switching hands on the tool easier. You can make a tether by girth-hitching a length of 9/16-inch webbing or 6mm perlon (either is anchor strength) to the axe leash and clipping this to your waist harness. Likewise, you can clip the tether to your chest harness, where it will be less in the way, but less handy for anchoring the axe at a belay. Either way, girth-hitching the tether to your piolet lets you quickly detach it when you step off the glacier and onto more technical terrain, where the tether would be in the way.

A webbing/bungy tether allows a good tether length and keeps the system neat without lots of dangly cord or webbing. To home make this item, thread some thin bungy cord into tubular webbing and stretch the bungy while tying an overhand-on-a-bight knot on either end. Then girth hitch one end to the head of your ice axe and clip the other to your harness.

ALPINE PICK
for SELF ARREST

NEGATIVE CLEARANCE

POSITIVE CLEARANCE

SPECIALIZED PICK
for STEEP ICE

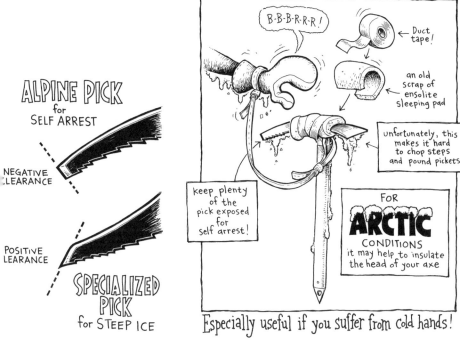

B·B·B·R·R·R!

← Duct tape!

an old scrap of ensolite sleeping pad

unfortunately, this makes it hard to chop steps and pound pickets

keep plenty of the pick exposed for self arrest!

FOR **ARCTIC** CONDITIONS
it may help to insulate the head of your axe

Especially useful if you suffer from cold hands!

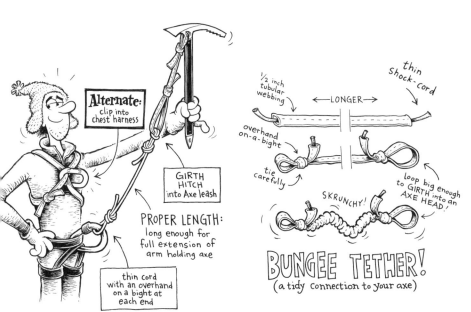

Alternate: clip into chest harness

GIRTH HITCH into Axe leash

PROPER LENGTH: long enough for full extension of arm holding axe

thin cord with an overhand on a bight at each end

½ inch tubular webbing

thin shock-cord

←LONGER→

overhand on-a-bight

tie carefully

loop big enough to GIRTH into an AXE HEAD!

SKRUNCHY!

BUNGEE TETHER!
(a tidy connection to your axe)

Knots

Here are all the knots necessary for the systems presented in this book. These are our favorites, and many others could be substituted, but as Mike says, "There are plenty of knot books out there — no need for another!"

The **Flemish bend** is used for joining two ropes together. It's also an excellent knot for tying your waist prusik cord in a loop.

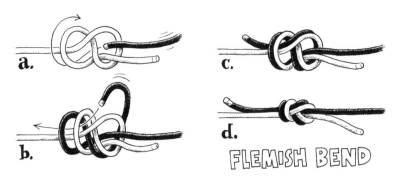

FLEMISH BEND

The **double fisherman's** is another good knot for joining two ropes together.

DOUBLE FISHERMAN

The **water knot** is a time-tested knot for tying together rope, cord, or webbing. It is simply an overhand knot with another overhand reversed through it. For safety, be sure to leave "tails" on the knot that are at least two inches long — longer is better, especially in webbing. Since this knot is prone to loosening and untying itself, load it with body weight to snug it down; wetting the knot and then weighting it will let it cinch up even tighter.

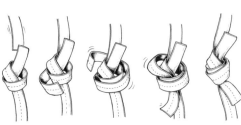

FIGURE 8 on a BIGHT

The **figure eight** on a bight is used extensively in climbing and mountaineering. It's very similar to an overhand (like you would tie in the top of a garbage bag) but the extra twist in it makes it easier to untie, and it is stronger.

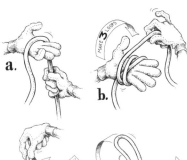

The **butterfly** is the classic middle-person knot. A figure eight on a bight also works for this, although it is not meant to have its tail ends pulled apart. The butterfly is designed to take a load in three directions, so it is an excellent knot for the middle of a rope team.

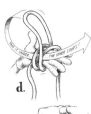
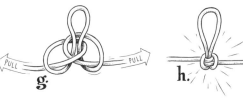

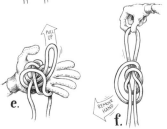

The **improved prusik hitch** is one of many 'friction hitches'. It is friendly on the rope and can be placed anywhere. It is light, simple, and cheap, with no moving parts. Get yours today! In this book we drop the word 'improved' throughout the text, though we always are referring to a three-wrap prusik hitch. This is not the technically correct term, though it is commonly understood as such.

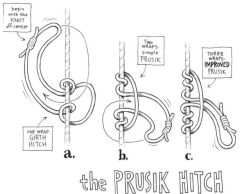

the PRUSIK HITCH

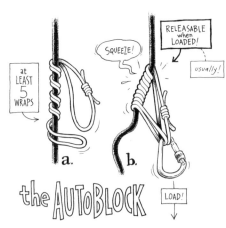

at LEAST 5 WRAPS

SQUEEZE!

RELEASABLE when LOADED!

usually!

a. b.

the AUTOBLOCK

LOAD!

The **Autoblock** is great 'friction hitch' that could be substituted for the 'ratchet prusik' setup used throughout the book. It is easy to tie and can usually be unloaded while weighted.

The **Munter hitch** is an excellent and simple hitch that you can use in place of a belay or rappel device, though it might kink the rope a little. The Munter is useful for making rescue systems reversible. All it requires is a large locking carabiner ("pear" carabiners work best).

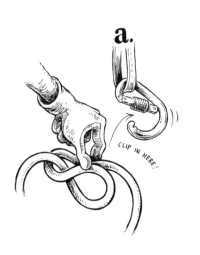

a.

CLIP IN HERE!

b.

BRAKE HAND

feeding rope OUT

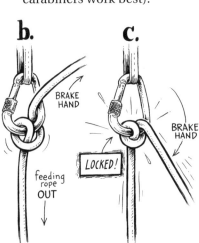

c.

BRAKE HAND

LOCKED!

The **Munter with a mule hitch** is a very effective way to tie off the Munter hitch so that you can let go of your brake hand. This hitch should be backed up with an overhand knot (e).

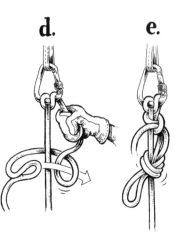

d.

e.

f.

CLI the t into t ANCH

24

Pack leash

A crevasse fall with a big pack is brutal. You can't do anything but suffer until you dump your pack. You'll need to jettison quickly without losing it. Pre-rig your pack with a tether, but first make sure the pack's haul loop is stout enough to hold a load. If it isn't, reinforce it by tying a sling around the shoulder straps. Clip the tether to the sling and the haul loop. The tether itself can simply be the tail end of the rope you're clipped to, or a three-foot sling.

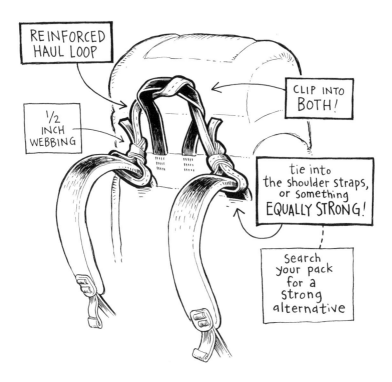

REINFORCED HAUL LOOP

1/2 INCH WEBBING

CLIP INTO BOTH!

tie into the shoulder straps, or something EQUALLY STRONG!

Search your pack for a strong alternative

Prusiks, ascenders, and cordelettes

Set foot on a glacier and you'll need a rescue system based on friction hitches (prusiks) or mechanical ascenders, such as those made by Jumar, Gibbs, and Petzl. You'll employ prusiks or ascenders for various tasks, from climbing a rope out of a crevasse after you've fallen in, to rigging a ratcheting haul system to extract your partner from a crevasse.

Prusiks are lightweight, simple, inexpensive, multi-directional (hold a load from any direction), usually grip icy ropes, and and don't damage your rope. Prusiks are, however, more difficult to get on and off the rope than mechanical ascenders, and aren't as easy to operate, especially when you're wearing mittens. Conversely, ascenders are easy to snap off and on the rope and are simple to operate even when your hands are ensconced in gloves. Ascenders are heavy, don't work as well in icy conditions, and can accidentally pop off the rope, sometimes because the safety catch wasn't properly engaged to begin with. Ascenders can also damage your rope if used to hold or catch large loads.

Weighing the pros and cons of prusiks and ascenders, we recommend prusiks for general mountaineering. The basic glacier rig is two prusik loops — one "waist" prusik and one "foot" prusik — hitched on the rope and clipped to your harness. For the waist prusik, take a five- to seven-foot piece of 6mm perlon tied in a loop with a double fisherman's or Flemish bend (page 22). This loop is then hitched onto the rope and clipped to a locking carabiner on your waist harness. This cord is known as the "waist" prusik.

To make the foot prusik, take a second piece of perlon and tie as shown in the illustrations on pages 28 and 29. (Note: prusik lengths are given based on a waist harness. You'll need to adjust lengths to use with a full-body harness.) When you're finished and both prusiks are on the rope, you'll end up with a dangling foot loop. Stuff this out of the way, either in a pocket or under your harness. Or just clip it to your harness with a spare carabiner.

ooops!

IMPORTANT! make sure your pack leash ain't too long...

Don't clip your ascending gear to your pack... if you drop your pack it'll be really hard to retrieve!

If you use mechanical ascenders — perhaps you're carrying them anyway for a climb — girth hitch a sling to your harness, clip this to the ascender, and clip the ascender to your gear sling, where it will ride at the ready as a "waist" ascender. Your second ascender is your foot rig, and is attached to you using the foot prusik previously mentioned: girth hitch the ascender to the sling's middle loop, and clip the whole thing to your gear sling, ready for use.

ROPE DAMAGE!

most HARD CAM units use tiny sharp teeth that can **MUNCH** a rope during a shock-loading event!

a soft PRUSIK HITCH is an easy and excellent alternative

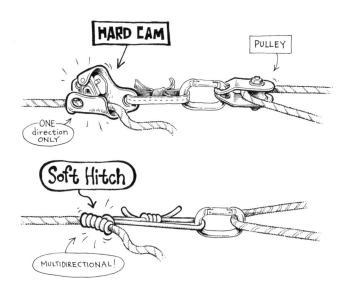

HARD CAM

PULLEY

ONE direction ONLY

Soft Hitch

MULTIDIRECTIONAL!

Using two mechanical ascenders (or jugs) like you would on a big wall is overkill. It's impractical and unnecessary for glacier travel. Never travel with mechanical ascenders on the rope — the shock load of a fall will cause the teeth of the ascender to rip your rope, and the ascenders will clonk you in the face if you fall in a crevasse.

Another essential is a cordelette, a 20-foot loop of 7mm cord tied with a double fisherman's knot to form a loop. The cordelette simplifies any anchor rigging; every glacier traveler should carry one. Another option is to bring a 10- to 12-foot Webolette, which is a piece of webbing with sewn loops on either end.

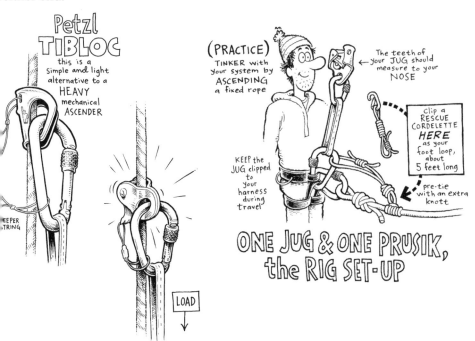

Petzl TIBLOC
this is a simple and light alternative to a HEAVY mechanical ASCENDER

KEEPER STRING

LOAD

(PRACTICE)
TINKER with your system by ASCENDING a fixed rope

The teeth of your JUG should measure to your NOSE

Clip a RESCUE CORDELETTE HERE as your foot loop, about 5 feet long

pre-tie with an extra knott

KEEP the JUG clipped to your harness during travel

ONE JUG & ONE PRUSIK, the RIG SET-UP

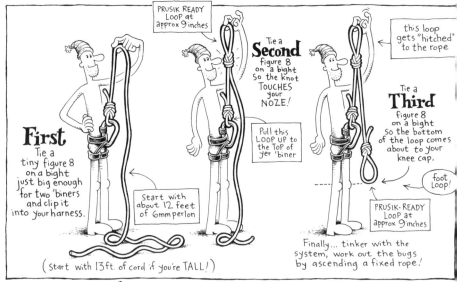

~ tying the foot prusik ~

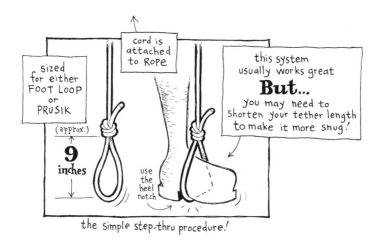

the simple step-thru procedure!

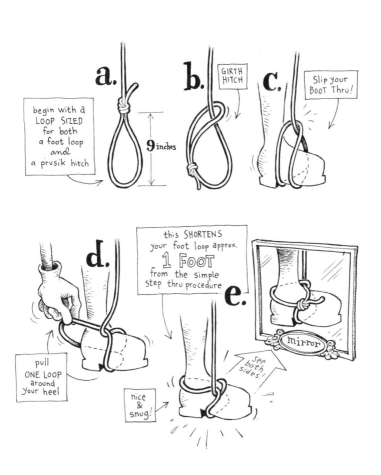

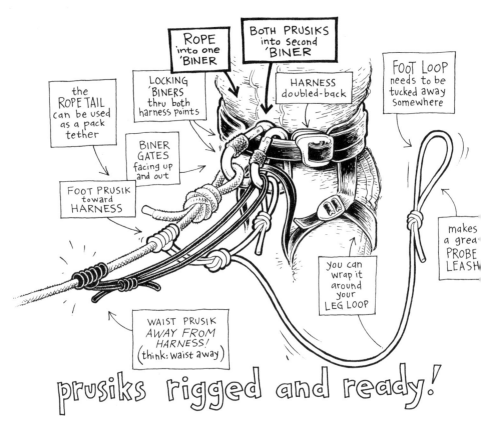

ROPE into one 'BINER

BOTH PRUSIKS into second 'BINER

the ROPE TAIL can be used as a pack tether

LOCKING 'BINERS thru both harness points

HARNESS doubled-back

FOOT LOOP needs to be tucked away somewhere

BINER GATES facing up and out

FOOT PRUSIK toward HARNESS

makes a grea PROBE LEASH

WAIST PRUSIK AWAY FROM HARNESS! (think: waist away)

you can wrap it around your LEG LOOP

prusiks rigged and ready!

Pulleys

Pulleys are not necessary equipment although one or two pulleys will make hauling some-one out of a crevasse a little easier than simply running the rope through carabiners. Shop for a pulley that is lightweight, has internal bearings, and is designed to handle heavy loads. Avoid super lightweight or "emergency" pulleys — these typically don't work much better than carabin-ers. Also avoid the large, heavy pulleys designed for search-and-rescue missions and the "wall-hauler" type ratcheting pulleys.

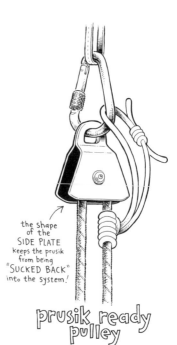

the shape of the SIDE PLATE keeps the prusik from being "SUCKED BACK" into the system!

prusik ready pulley

Snowshoes or skis?

Any glacier travel in the winter or big, cold mountain travel in the summer will likely require snowshoes or skis to prevent you from sinking chest deep in snow. Skis and snowshoes offer roughly the same flotation and will climb slopes of similar steepness. Of the two, skis are certainly faster and more exciting on the descent, provided it's good skiing terrain, and distribute your weight over a larger area, reducing your chances of punching through a snow-covered crevasse. Skis are also heavier than snowshoes, require a much higher level of skill to use, and are challenging to maneuver in crevasse fields and on narrow ridges. Skis are, of course, ideal for ski tours; but they're awful to carry up climbing routes, and especially bad for bushwhacking, where snowshoes are decidedly superior.

Skis

You have two choices for skis: randonee or tele. Randonee (or alpine touring, "AT") skis are basically short, metal-edged downhill skis, great for mountaineering because even a rudimentary downhill skier can manage them. Better still, most plastic and leather climbing boots fit AT bindings. The down side: mountaineering boots are too "soft" to give you much control over your skis, turning low-angle downhills into survival runs. For optimal skiing performance you'll need a specialized AT boot with a flexible cuff that enables you to climb, and a lock that secures the cuff, yielding control for downhill skiing. AT boots are, however, usually heavier, bulkier, and more expensive than climbing boots. As a rule of thumb, choose climbing boots when the route involves actual climbing, and AT boots for outings where you'll rarely take off your skis.

CONSIDER DE-TUNING YOUR EDGES to prevent ROPE DAMAGE!

Tele boots are more flexible than AT boots, making them more comfortable for long ski tours. Problems: Tele boots, while they will hold crampons, are awkward to climb in. And turning tele skis requires specific training and practice, things you can't pick up on your own, on the fly.

To determine which type of ski is best you must evaluate your skiing level. If you can't tele ski, AT is the only way for you. If you can tele ski — and well enough to do so in a rope team on a glacier — then evaluate whether your objective is skiing or climbing. Climbing goals will generally require AT gear. Skiing objectives can be accomplished with either type of gear.

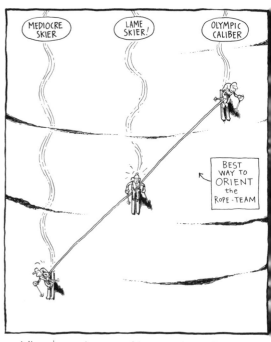

Ski skins

Skins are hairy strips that attach to ski bottoms, allowing them to grip on the uphills but slide on the downhills. Skins are a necessity, and there are three types: natural hair (mohair), synthetic hair, and plastic "snake skins" that buckle to your skis. Mohair skins are the most expensive, so most people opt for either synthetic hair or plastic. Synthetic skins use glue to hold them to your skis; over time the glue wears out — though it can be replaced. Since plastic skins attach via buckles, there's no glue to cause a problem. Plastic skins, however, break more often and don't climb as well. All in all, synthetic skins are your best bet.

When descending on skis try to keep the rope at about a 45° angle for better control

Climbing Skins

Some folks count on the excellent flotation of their skis to keep them out of crevasses and skip the rope, especially if they are out in the winter or early spring when there is still lots of snow covering everything. Obviously this is a safety gamble. For the conservative among us, roped skiing is the way to go.

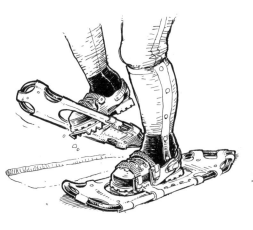

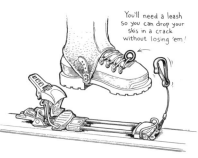

You'll need a leash so you can drop your skis in a crack without losing 'em!

Regardless of your skiing skills, rope up and you will soon ski over your rope, which, if your skis have sharp metal edges, will soon look like it went through a blender. Save your rope by filing down your edges so they are dull.

Uphill roped skiing with skins is no mystery; it's the downhill that's the challenge. It might help to keep your skins on. These will slow you, but can also "high center" your skis, preventing the metal edges from fully engaging the snow.

Rope management and skiing are a difficult combination. Keep in mind that your primary concern is staying out of crevasses. Forget about making perfect turns and concentrate on keeping slack out of the rope — not an easy thing. If you are skiing in the lead, be sure to alert your partner well before you stop. Sudden stops will cause your partner to run up on you, putting a giant loop of slack in the rope. Other tips: Ski at 45-degree angles to one another to keep the rope out from under foot; put the best skier last on the rope, where he can control the rope's slack or tension; and have the last skier ski with his skins on. The skins will slow that skier, braking the entire group.

DON'T LOSE 'EM!

Snowshoes

Snowshoes are lighter weight and easier to pack and carry than skis. They are also more maneuverable (a plus in crevasse fields), work with any sort of footwear, and require no skill. If you can walk, you can snowshoe.

Disadvantages of snowshoes: They are great for going forward and up, but can skate out from under you on downhills and traversing slopes.

Snowshoes can also break under the stresses of heavy packs. Bring a repair kit and be ready to improvise. Plastic "zip ties" and parachute cord are indispensable for almost all snowshoe repairs.

If you decide on snowshoes, select a pair with aggressive crampons and enough surface area to float you and your pack in the type of snow you'll likely encounter. The softer the snow and the heavier your weight, the larger the snowshoe you'll need. "Heel lifts" are super useful and found on some newer snow shoes.

For snowshoes and skis alike, you'll need retaining straps that, in the event you fall in a crevasse, let you quickly detach the skis or snowshoes and not lose them.

Or, if you're going to the North Cascades in July, rejoice and leave the skis and snowshoes at home!

Clothing

It may be roasting hot on the surface of a glacier, but inside a crevasse it is freezing and wet. Wear clothing that will protect you from the blazing sun, yet keep you warm in a crevasse. Hypothermia will only complicate a rescue.

Gloves or mittens are necessary for all glacier travel. Arresting a crevasse fall requires your hands. Bare hands in snow just don't cut it — if you have an ice axe in your hand, you need gloves. If it's hot, thin gloves are fine.

Mitten and glove shells are not waterproof in the rain, no matter what the manufacturer says. Your hands will get wet. No big deal, just don't spend a lot for "water-proof gloves."

always: IF YOU ARE USING AN **ICE AXE,** WEAR GLOVES!

without hand protection, arresting a fall can be excruciating!

HIGH NOON ON THE GLACIER

Thank goodness I brought my favorite shorts!

TEMP

ONE half SECOND LATER...

TEMP

Don't skimp on warm head layers. In cold weather a wool or synthetic cap or balaclava, which also covers your neck, are standard issue. A bandanna/baseball cap combo offers great protection from the sun.

Wear light-colored synthetic long underwear. Light colors are cool in the sun, and the synthetic fabric will insulate even when it's wet.

A simple, windproof nylon shell jacket with a hood and pants trap heat well, shed snow, and aren't too sweaty. Many super-tricked-out shell jackets and bibs are overkill, heavy, and expensive. If in doubt, err on the cheap, lightweight side.

I've seen faces fry like crispy bacon in the 24-hour daylight of Alaska. Sun protection is imperative in the high-UV environment of a glacier. Apply sunscreen to your face and neck every two to four hours. Also, prevent snowblindness by wearing dark sunglasses with 100-percent UVA and UVB protection. The best glacier goggles have a nose guard and side shields for added protection. Throw fashion out the window and leave your svelte hipster sunglasses at home, you only get two eyes — don't sizzle 'em.

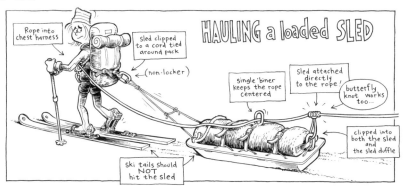

Sleds

Skip the sled if you can. A sled may be your friend for hauling large loads on big, flat glaciers, but is otherwise cumbersome and problematic to maneuver. In the event a sled is a must, here are tips for lessening the pain:

• Keep the load at 80 pounds, maximum. Make it heaviest in the middle to back so the front doesn't auger into the snow.

• Tie a length of thick (11mm) rope to the front of the sled and have the sled run over this rope on downhills. The friction from the rope will act as a brake.

• Secure everything to the sled so you don't lose anything in a routine sled pile up or major crevasse fall.

• Clip the team's rope through a carabiner on top of the sled to keep the sled from running over it.

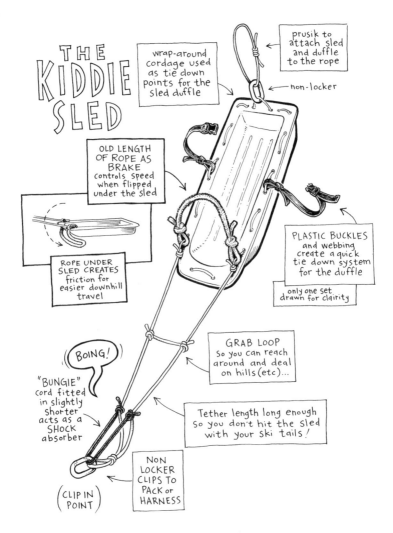

THE KIDDIE SLED

wrap-around cordage used as tie down points for the sled duffle

prusik to attach sled and duffle to the rope

non-locker

OLD LENGTH OF ROPE AS BRAKE controls speed when flipped under the sled

ROPE UNDER SLED CREATES friction for easier downhill travel

PLASTIC BUCKLES and webbing create a quick tie down system for the duffle

only one set drawn for clairity

GRAB LOOP So you can reach around and deal on hills (etc)...

BOING!

"BUNGIE" cord fitted in slightly shorter acts as a SHOCK absorber

Tether length long enough So you don't hit the sled with your ski tails!

NON LOCKER CLIPS TO PACK or HARNESS

(CLIP IN POINT)

• Attach the back of the sled (and load) to the rope-team rope to prevent it from bonking you on the head if you fall in a crevasse. A prusik loop or butterfly knot works well for this attachment.

• The middle person and/or first person on a rope should pull the sled, while the following person helps control it on sidehills and descents.

The whole shebang

The illustrations on page 37 show the end and middle persons rigged for travel. Note how they are attached to all of their stuff. These illustrations make it look like all of the slings and gear fit neatly and comfortably when you're wearing a big pack, but they don't. The pack hipbelt ends up sitting on top of your harness, with the buckle above your waist carabiners. If you take your pack off, be careful to put it back on so that it is in the right place and not covering tethers and ropes. Also left out are snowshoes or skis, wands, transceivers, probe-pole tether, and all of the other crazy stuff you might need.

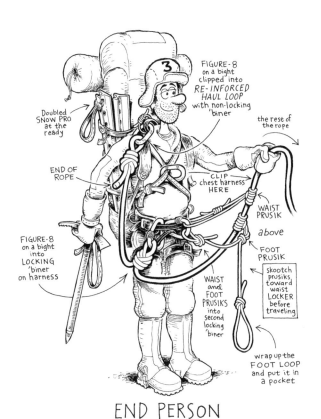

FIGURE-8 on a bight clipped into *RE-INFORCED HAUL LOOP* with non-locking 'biner

3

Doubled SNOW PRO at the ready

END OF ROPE

the rest of the rope

CLIP chest harness HERE

WAIST PRUSIK

above

FOOT PRUSIK

skootch prusiks toward waist LOCKER before traveling

FIGURE-8 on a bight into LOCKING 'biner on harness

WAIST and FOOT PRUSIKS into second locking 'biner

wrap up the FOOT LOOP and put it in a pocket

END PERSON

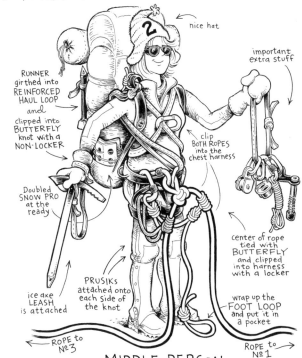

2

nice hat

important extra stuff

RUNNER girthed into REINFORCED HAUL LOOP *and* clipped into BUTTERFLY knot with a NON-LOCKER

clip BOTH ROPES into the chest harness

Doubled SNOW PRO at the ready

center of rope tied with BUTTERFLY and clipped into harness with a locker

ice axe LEASH is attached

PRUSIKS attached onto each side of the knot

wrap up the FOOT LOOP and put it in a pocket

ROPE to №3

ROPE to №1

MIDDLE PERSON

Safety Checking

With all this stuff on, including bulky layers and early morning, it's necessary to do a complete safety check with your teammates. This will give you peace of mind that your system is rigged correctly and everything is in order. They'll need to do the same for you. This is an excellent habit and should be done every time you venture out into crevassed terrain. It's all too common to find a mistake during these checks.

CHECK:
1. Harness tight and buckle doubled back.
2. Locking biner though both waist and leg loops.
3. Rope has a good knot and is clipped into locking biner.
4. Prusiks attached correctly and clipped into the other locking biner.
5. Biners locked.
6. Rope runs through the chest harness.
7. Pack tether attached.
8. Ice axe leash on wrist or attached.
9. Enough extra gear and pro to perform a rescue.
10. Sled rigged and ready.

Gear check list

Most of this gear is mandatory to travel safely on a glacier. Obviously a weekend jaunt up Mount Hood and an expedition to Ulugh Muztagh will have different requirements — adjust your gear as necessary.

CLIMBING AND TRAVEL
- ❏ Ice axes
- ❏ Crampons
- ❏ Snowshoes
- ❏ Skis and skins
- ❏ Sleds or drag bags
- ❏ Sled/cache duffels
- ❏ Probes
- ❏ Wands
- ❏ Pickets
- ❏ Flukes
- ❏ Ice screws
- ❏ Rock pro
- ❏ Pulley(s)
- ❏ Ascenders
- ❏ Non-locking carabiners
- ❏ Locking carabiners
- ❏ Prusik cords
- ❏ Webbing
- ❏ Extra perlon/prusik
- ❏ Sunscreen

CAMPING/COOKING
- ❏ Repair kit
- ❏ First-aid kit
- ❏ Tent and stakes
- ❏ Snow shovels
- ❏ Snow saws
- ❏ Poop bags
- ❏ Pots and fry pans
- ❏ Spatulas, cook spoons, pot grips
- ❏ Stoves
- ❏ Stove pads
- ❏ Fuel bottles
- ❏ Chocolate

PERSONAL CLOTHING
- ❏ Head system (sun hat, warm hat, bandanna, glacier glasses)
- ❏ Hand system (mitten shells, wool/pile gloves, liner gloves)
- ❏ Foot system (boots, bootie system, camp shoes)
- ❏ Upper-body layers (wind, rain, insulating, underwear)
- ❏ Lower-body layers (wind, rain, insulating, underwear)

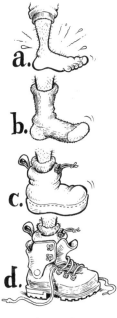

a.

b.

c.

d.

e.

f.

g.

WARM &
DRY FEET!

CAREFUL!
Don't damage
the leash!

HIT with
the FLAT
PART of
the ADZE!

HAMMER-
SHMAMMER!

KLONK!

RELIABLE?
Only if
the snow is
REALLY HARD!
i.e. "picket snow")

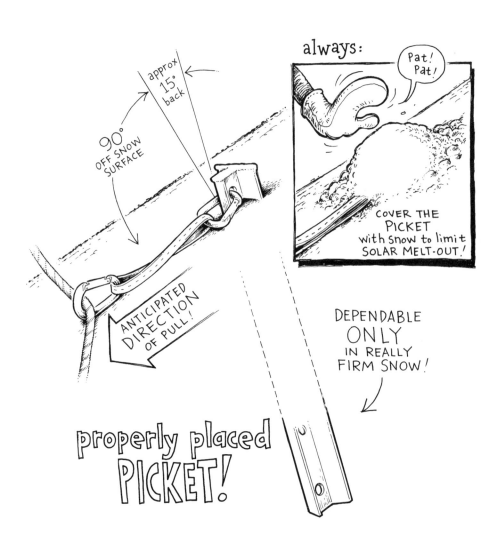

always:

Pat! Pat!

COVER THE PICKET with snow to limit SOLAR MELT-OUT!

90° OFF SNOW SURFACE

approx 15° back

ANTICIPATED DIRECTION OF PULL!

DEPENDABLE ONLY IN REALLY FIRM SNOW!

properly placed PICKET!

there ain't nothing dainty about
WORK HARDENING SNOW
for a buried deadman!

Y ou're on a glacier, so almost all of your protection will either be placed in or constructed from snow and ice. Since snow and ice vary in condition and reliability from one hour to the next, getting good protection depends on your ability to evaluate conditions and select the most suitable form of protection.

Snow pickets

Essentially over-sized tent pegs, snow pickets are versatile pieces of snow protection. When the snow is firm, you can hammer one straight down, tent-peg style. When the snow is soft, you bury the picket horizontally. A good rule of thumb: If you have to pound in the picket with your ice axe, then the conditions are good for a vertical placement; if the snow is soft enough for you to push in the picket with your hand or foot, a horizontal placement is in order. In both cases clear away the soft, top layer of snow to reach more solid stuff underneath.

To place a vertical picket, hold the picket perpendicular to the snow surface, then tilt it up slope about 15 degrees. Using your ice hammer or the head of your ice axe, pound in the picket like a nail. Stop pounding when either the picket's top carabiner hole is even with the snow surface or the picket refuses to drive deeper. Clip a runner to the carabiner hole closest to the snow, or girth hitch a sling around the picket to tie it off. Note: Hammering the picket so the runner buries into the snow causes the runner to lever on the snow, weakening the placement. If you decide to "bury" the placement, cut a slot that lets the runner track out of the snow. If possible, cover the picket with snow to avoid solar melt out.

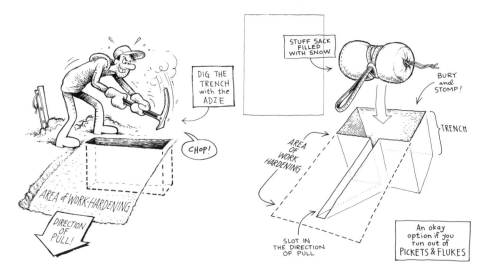

DIG THE TRENCH with the ADZE

CHOP!

AREA of WORK-HARDENING

DIRECTION OF PULL!

STUFF SACK FILLED WITH SNOW

BURY and STOMP!

TRENCH

AREA OF WORK HARDENING

SLOT IN THE DIRECTION OF PULL

An okay option if you run out of PICKETS & FLUKES

Deadmen

A deadman is any piece of gear — pickets, rocks, skis, stuff sacks filled with snow, backpacks, snowshoes — that you tie off and bury horizontally in the snow. Deadmanning is your ace in the hole for almost all snow conditions.

Two things determine a deadman's strength: snow conditions and the structural integrity of the deadmanned item. Ski poles, for example, might bend then break under a very heavy load, but they are better than nothing in a pinch.

To place a deadman, first visualize your direction of pull and where the picket needs to be in relation to the potential load. "Work harden" a three-foot square placement area by stomping it down as hard as possible. At the back or uphill side of this area, dig a trench at least one and a half feet deep. Then use the adze or pick of your axe to dig a "T" slot for the runner. Be sure to dig the trench and slot the same depth where they connect. Girth hitch the

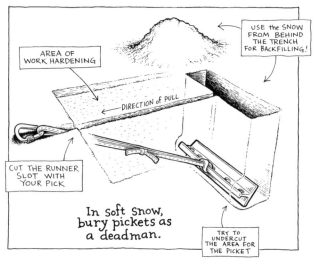

AREA OF WORK HARDENING

USE the SNOW FROM BEHIND THE TRENCH FOR BACKFILLING!

DIRECTION of PULL

CUT THE RUNNER SLOT WITH YOUR PICK

In soft snow, bury pickets as a deadman.

TRY TO UNDERCUT THE AREA FOR THE PICKET

center of the deadman with a sling. Place the deadman in the trench and run the webbing along the slot. Fill in the back trench with snow (don't take any from your work-hardened platform). Also fill in the "T" slot a bit, but don't mess with the work-hardened area. Clip your rope into the webbing and you are ready to go.

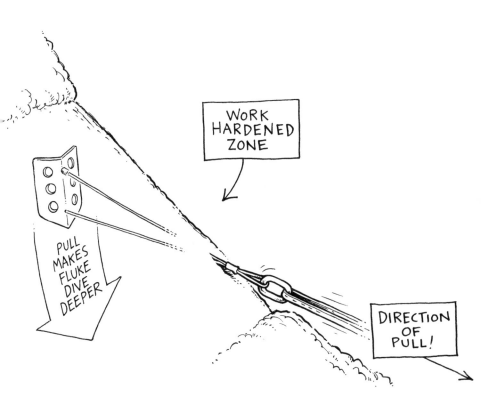

WORK
HARDENED
ZONE

PULL
MAKES
FLUKE
DIVE
DEEPER

DIRECTION
OF
PULL!

Flukes

These are aluminum plates that you slot into the snow, similar to a dead-man. When you weight a fluke, its angled design causes it to plow deeper into the snow, increasing its holding power. Unfortunately, if a fluke is placed improperly or hits an ice layer within the snowpack, it can zip right out of the snow. Obviously the nature of the snowpack and placement of the fluke are critical. If the snowpack has ice layers, use a picket instead of a fluke.

To place a fluke: Work-harden an area about three feet square. At the back of this square, use your ice-axe pick and make a single deep cut across the slope (perpendicular to the fall line). Angle this cut 45 degrees away from perpendicular to the snow slope. Then, take your pick and cut a "T" toward the anticipated direction of loading. Set the fluke in the first cut with the wire slotted into the T slot. Tap in the fluke with the head of your axe. Last, "set" the fluke by hooking its clip-in wire with your axe pick and giving it a yank in the anticipated direction of pull. Placing a fluke is much faster then placing a deadmaned picket and may be as strong in certain snow conditions. Plus, flukes are easier and less cumbersome to wear on your harness.

When you are setting an equalized anchor, keep in mind that a fluke moves under load. All of the force will shift onto the other anchors, giving you the reverse of the desired effect.

Ice screws

Alpine and glacier ice tends to have more air in it than the ice you find on a frozen waterfall. Even this airy and sometimes jigsaw-puzzle-like structure can usually yield screw placements. Typically, you can find solid ice under the junk by chopping away the surface ice. The best way to learn about ice is to place lots of screws and observe how easy or difficult they are to place in different conditions. The plug of ice that extrudes out of the screw is somewhat of a strength indicator. If this plug is consistent and dense, the placement is probably strong.

Since glacier ice may have a weak surface layer, the longer style screws are the way to go. "Shorty" screws (under 19 cm) can work, but might not penetrate the junky surface ice.

How much pro do you carry?

Even for flat, non-technical glacier travel, you'll need some gear in the event of a crevasse fall. The minimum for each person is one piece of snow or ice pro, a long cordelette or runner (for building an anchor), a short cordelette (for use as a prusik), and four carabiners. Increase the amount of snow and ice protection as the terrain warrants. If everyone has this minimal amount, the group can pool the gear in an emergency and have more than enough. Carry this gear on a simple, knotted, over-the-shoulder sling. For obvious reasons, don't let one person carry all of the gear.

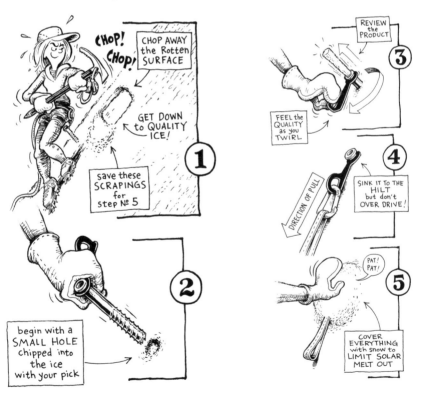

44

Ice threads

These are strong, require minimal gear, and are easy to construct. Ice threads also let you rappel an ice wall and only leave behind a sling. Great for glacier travel, ice threads do take more time to build than placing an ice screw, a consideration in emergency situations where time is critical.

To make an ice thread, clear a one-foot-square area down to solid, unfractured ice. Place an ice screw at a 45-degree angle to the surface, and fully sink it (you may need to chip away more ice to allow the hanger to turn). Remove the screw and place it again at a 45 degree angle to the ice, aiming for the bottom of the first screw hole. Remove this screw and you'll be left with a continuous tunnel in the ice. The more ice you can "capture" between the placements, the stronger the resulting protection. Last, take a piece of coat hanger (a toothbrush, stick, or Stopper are good substitutes) and fish a length of sling or cord through the tunnel. Tie the cord or sling in a loop using a ring bend. When in doubt, use two threads for redundancy.

FLAT WEBBING comfortable under your pack!

adjustable

45

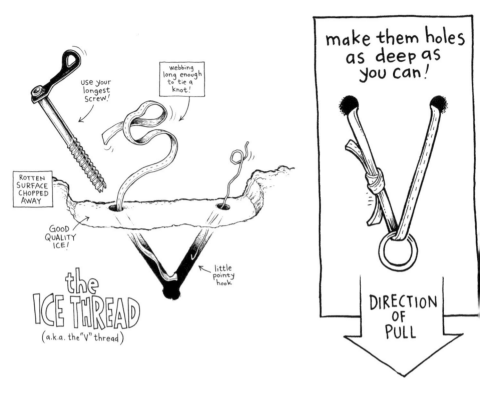

use your longest screw!

webbing long enough to tie a knot!

ROTTEN SURFACE CHOPPED AWAY

GOOD QUALITY ICE!

the
ICE THREAD
(a.k.a. the "V" thread)

little pointy hook

DIRECTION OF PULL

Bollards

Take a large chunk of solid snow, cut a trench around it, and you have a bollard that you can sling and use as an anchor. Like the ice thread, the bollard requires little gear, though it is time and labor intensive. Also like the ice thread, a bollard's strength depends on that of its medium. Hard or work-hardened (stomped-down) snow is imperative. A bollard's size varies significantly depending on the snow conditions. In soft snow a bollard might need to be 10 feet in diameter; in hard snow a one-and-a-half-foot bollard may suffice.

To make a bollard, work-harden an area five to 10 feet in diameter. Carve a trench in a modified teardrop shape with the fat end on the uphill side. The back or uphill side of the bollard should be the deepest part of the trench and is the most important part. Make this part of the trench at least one and a half feet deep, and slightly incut so it'll hold a sling or rope. The side trenches should become shallower until the downhill tip, which should be near the snow surface.

To prevent the rope or sling from cheese-wiring through the snow, pad the back of the bollard. Rocks, ice axes, or stuff sacks work well. Finally, drop your rope or sling in the trench around the bollard. If you are using webbing, tie a loop in its downhill end to prevent it from shifting and sawing into the bollard. If you are using your rope to rappel, place the knot to one side near the tip of the teardrop.

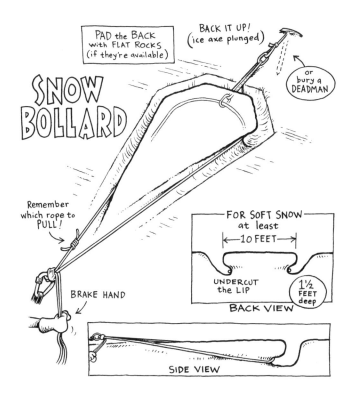

SNOW BOLLARD

PAD the BACK with FLAT ROCKS (if they're available)

BACK IT UP! (ice axe plunged)

or bury a DEADMAN

Remember which rope to PULL!

BRAKE HAND

FOR SOFT SNOW at least
|←—10 FEET—→|

UNDERCUT the LIP

1½ FEET deep

BACK VIEW

SIDE VIEW

Tip: When you rappel off a bollard, the rope can pressure-melt into place, making it difficult to retrieve. When this happens, weight both ends of the rope, then let go of one end while continuing to pull on the other. The sudden unweighting should cause the rope to recoil and break free. For pesky stuck ropes, get the whole team pulling.

Watch out!

Solar melt out and pressure melting will weaken any placement in snow or ice, but are particular concerns for screws and pickets.

Solar melt out: The sun heats the metal, which in turn melts the ice or snow surrounding it, causing a loose anchor. This can happen in any

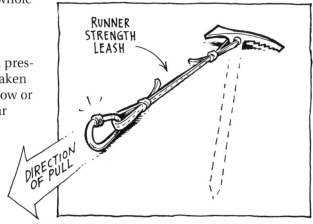

RUNNER STRENGTH LEASH

DIRECTION OF PULL

GOOD PROTECTION **ONLY** in high quality hard snow!

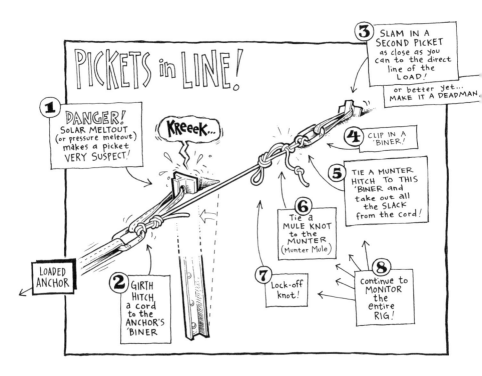

temperature. To minimize solar melt out, cover the placement with a mound of ice or snow. Keep in mind that burying the piece only slows solar melt out — UV rays penetrate snow, so the placement will still melt out. Get in the habit of regularly checking your fixed anchors.

Pressure melting: When you load an anchor, the pressure from your weight melts the snow or ice around the anchor, reducing its strength. Prevent this by keeping your weight off the anchor. At belays, for example, chop a stance and stand there instead of hanging on the anchors.

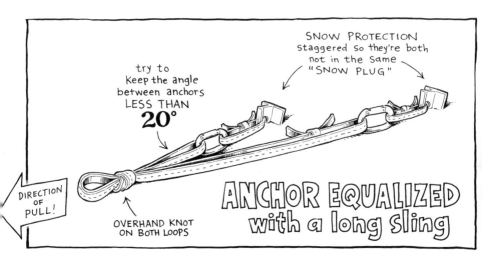

Putting it all together

On a glacier you'll use three types of anchor systems. The most basic is a single piece of protection like a picket or ice axe, combined with good position, such as a solid snow-seat belay. Simple anchors such as these are, in firm snow, usually adequate to belay your partner across a tricky spot.

When a long, hard fall is a real possibility you need a more substantial belay anchor: two or more pieces that are each strong enough to hold your entire team, plus any additional load caused by shock loading. These belay anchors must be equalized so they share the load evenly, and should be tied off so if one piece pulls the other won't be shock loaded. A redundant, equalized, tied-off system is almost infallible. You are safe even if one piece or its connecting sling fails. This type of anchor is used for crevasse rescue. It is composed of a minimum of two pieces of equalized pro, such as two deadmanned pickets. Each point of protection has a piece of webbing or cord clipped or hitched to it that extends toward the crevasse. The illustration shows two deadmanned pickets joined by a standard cordelette. Note that the cordelette forms a "master point." The master point is where you attach the crevasse victim's rope. More on that later.

The third anchor type is that used for rappelling. A single large bollard deadmanned rock, or ice thread may be used. A rappel anchor needs to hold at least twice your body weight, yet use minimal gear.

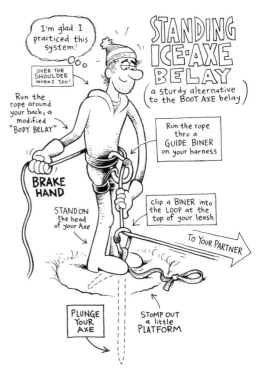

49

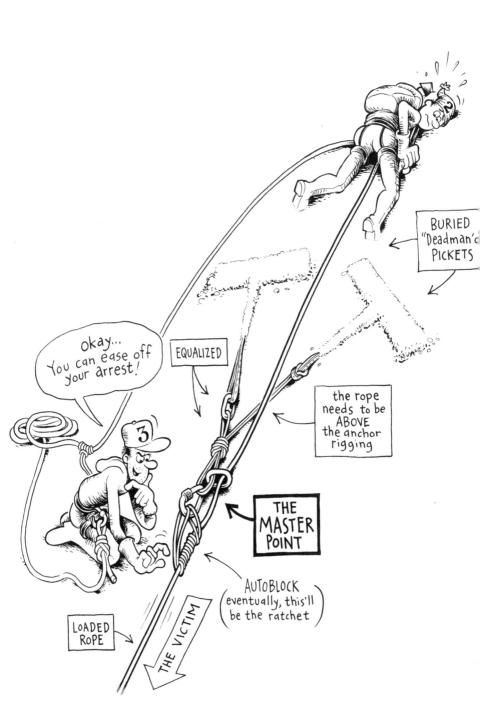

Roping up lets us travel together, ready to work as a team in case of a fall. This is not a casual undertaking. When we rope together we trust each other with our lives. Tying into a rope starts a relationship and a system. We cannot go anywhere or do anything without it affecting the others on the rope. This means good communication is paramount. The system relies on our diligence and attention as well. We must keep slack out of the rope, change our orientation to hazards when appropriate, and place running pro when necessary. If we don't pay attention, remain diligent, and communicate well, the rope will be detrimental; it could even lead to death.

Often, holding a crevasse fall can be surprisingly gentle ... *but don't count on it!*

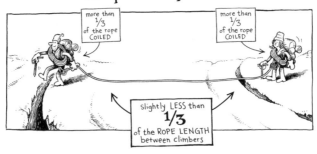

Forming teams

A rope team of three or four people is ideal for several reasons. If one person falls in a crevasse there are at least two people to arrest the fall. The communication and coordination of this small team is also reasonable, and the spacing between climbers is far enough that the rope's safety net can be properly used — i.e., one person at a time on a snow bridge and lots of rope to absorb a fall.

With five on a rope the distance between people is so short it is possible for two rope mates to be on the same snow bridge at once — not good. Communication and coordination also become problematic, though there are plenty of folks to arrest a fall and perform a crevasse rescue. Six or more on a rope is only recommended for emergency situations, or through known terrain.

Experienced mountaineers commonly travel on a glacier as a team of two. Novice glacier travelers, however, should stick to ropes of three or four where there's always two people to drop into self-arrest and assist with crevasse rescue. On a rope team of two, there is no back up! You have to arrest your partner's fall, rig anchors, transfer your weight onto these anchors, extract your partner, and administer first aid all by yourself.

When you form a rope team consider the physical size of each team member and, when possible, the terrain you will be traveling. For instance,

IF YOU'RE ON A ROPE TEAM, ALWAYS BE ALERT!

REMEMBER! If running backward makes things WORSE, just ARREST!

it would be unwise to put Conan the Barbarian and Peewee Herman on a two-person rope team since Peewee would have trouble arresting Conan if he fell in a crevasse.

Dividing a rope for a team of four

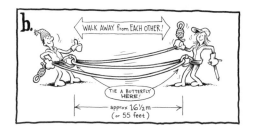

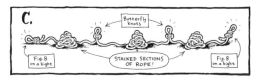

Dividing the rope

A two-person team will need extra rope for rescue purposes. To get this, two people should tie in using the figure-eight knot 45 feet apart, leaving each with 60 feet of extra rope (using a 165-foot or 50-meter rope), enough to reach a teammate in an emergency. Coil the two ends and carry them over your head and shoulder, or in a backpack.

On glaciers where the crevasses are more than 45 feet wide, a two-person team needs to put more than 45 feet of rope between them, or they risk falling into the same big hole. The simplest way to increase spacing on the rope is to use a longer 200 foot (60 m) rope, leaving 3 sections of 60 feet. Coil the 25 feet of slack on each end and tuck this in a pack or loop it over your shoulder, where you can access it for use during a crevasse rescue.

To divide a rope for a three-person team, start with a stacked rope, take both ends and pull the rope through your hands until you get to the middle. At the middle, tie a butterfly knot for the middle person. Tie a figure-eight on a bight at each end for the other two people. Everyone clips to his knot with at least one locking carabiner.

The illustrations opposite show a handy method for dividing a rope for a four-person team. Note that the end people clip in using figure-eight knots.

DIVIDING the ROPE!

2 PERSON TEAM

(coil it!)

CoILED!

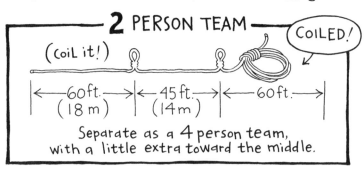

|←——60 ft.——→|←——45 ft.——→|←——60 ft.——→|
(18 m)   (14 m)

Separate as a **4** person team,
with a little extra toward the middle.

3 PERSON TEAM

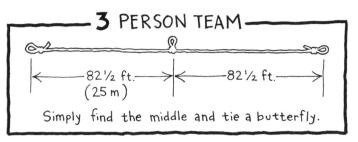

|←————82½ ft.————→|←————82½ ft.————→|
(25 m)

Simply find the middle and tie a butterfly.

4 PERSON TEAM

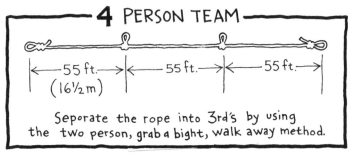

|←——55 ft.——→|←——55 ft.——→|←——55 ft.——→|
(16½ m)

Seperate the rope into 3rd's by using
the two person, grab a bight, walk away method.

5 PERSON TEAM

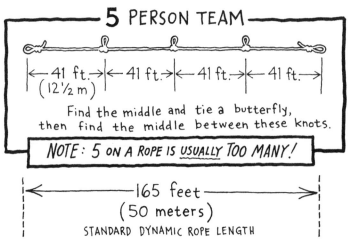

|←—41 ft.—→|←—41 ft.—→|←—41 ft.—→|←—41 ft.—→|
(12½ m)

Find the middle and tie a butterfly,
then find the middle between these knots.

NOTE : 5 ON A ROPE IS _USUALLY_ TOO MANY!

|←————————165 feet————————→|
(50 meters)
STANDARD DYNAMIC ROPE LENGTH

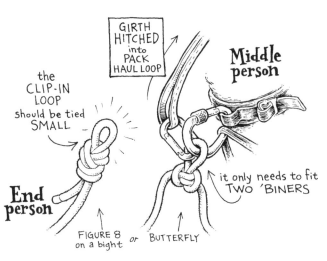

the **CLIP-IN LOOP** should be tied **SMALL**

End person

GIRTH HITCHED into PACK HAUL LOOP

Middle person

it only needs to fit **TWO 'BINERS**

FIGURE 8 on a bight *or* BUTTERFLY

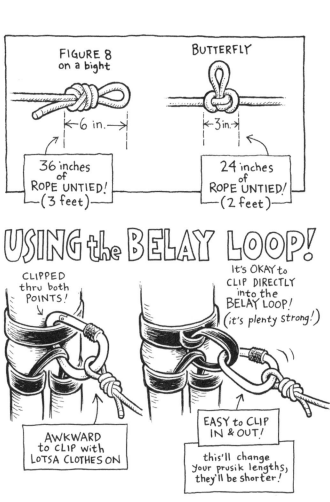

FIGURE 8 on a bight

←—6 in.—→

36 inches of ROPE UNTIED! (3 feet)

BUTTERFLY

←3 in.→

24 inches of ROPE UNTIED! (2 feet)

USING the BELAY LOOP!

CLIPPED thru both POINTS!

AWKWARD to CLIP with LOTSA CLOTHES ON

It's OKAY to CLIP DIRECTLY into the BELAY LOOP! (it's plenty strong!)

EASY to CLIP IN & OUT!

this'll change your prusik lengths, they'll be shorter!

CARRYING COILS ON YOUR PACK

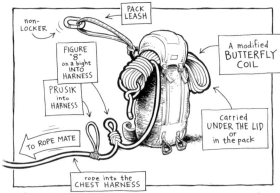

non-LOCKER

PACK LEASH

FIGURE "8" on a bight INTO HARNESS

A modified BUTTERFLY COIL

PRUSIK into HARNESS

TO ROPE MATE

carried UNDER THE LID or in the pack

rope into the CHEST HARNESS

this lets you easily remove your pack.

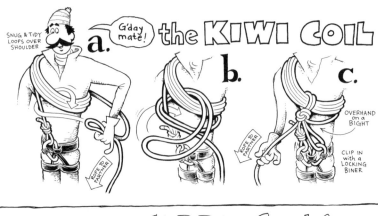

SNUG & TIDY LOOPS OVER SHOULDER

G'day mate! **a.** the **KIWI COIL**

b.

c.

ROPE TO PARTNER

ROPE TO PARTNER

OVERHAND on a BIGHT

CLIP IN with a LOCKING BINER

How to CARRY COILS:

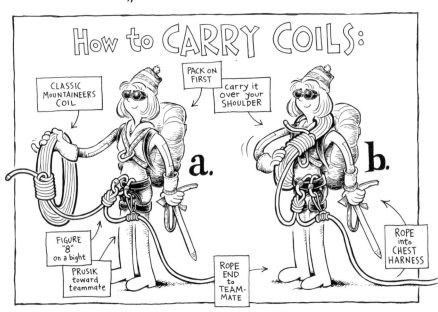

CLASSIC MOUNTAINEERS COIL

PACK ON FIRST

carry it over your SHOULDER

a.

b.

FIGURE "8" on a bight

PRUSIK toward teammate

ROPE END to TEAM-MATE

ROPE into CHEST HARNESS

Coiling rope ends

There are a few different ways to coil rope ends for carrying. A small butterfly coil works well if you are going to stuff it in the top of your pack. The mountaineering coil works well for carrying the rope over your head and shoulder while traveling without a pack. The Kiwi coil is another great way to carry coils.

Stack it!

The last step when dividing the rope is to stack it for travel. Start with the end that will leave last and stack it in the direction you'll be going. Set the knots aside so your rope mates can easily clip in.

a. OK!

b. GO! (CLEAR!)

c. STOP! (ZERO!)

Communicating with other rope teams over long distances needs to be simple and clear.

d. travel this DIRECTION!

e. DANGER!

Communication

Good teamwork requires good communication. Since wind and poor visibility typically hamper communication on a glacier, glacier travelers need a system that works in all conditions. The spoken commands "go" and "stop" certainly work, but the less-harsh sounding "clear" instead of go and "zero" instead of stop work well as long they are sounded loudly and clearly. It helps to repeat the commands for all to hear. The commands can be passed to other rope teams using the illustrated visual signals.

Keep slack out of the system

Too much slack between glacier travelers will add distance to a fall, while a tight rope will tug annoyingly on whoever is in front of you. Good rope management requires diligence, practice, and working together. Keeping the rope properly managed may mean you speed up, slow down, stop, or even back up. When you can't freely change position it is possible to use your prusik to take in slack, though it's best to only use this type of "belay" when absolutely necessary.

The rope should catch a fall, **NOT** your prusik!

DON'T LET YOUR ROPE DEVELOP A LONG LOOP OF SLACK!

Keep your prusik hitch skootched in close to your harness

Hmmm... what's the safest route?

№1 has no rope duties... HE IS ROUTE FINDING!

nice rope...

№2 has all the ROPE DUTIES for the rope ahead of her

№3 has the DUTIES of the rope ahead (PLUS) a good overview of the entire team!

Limit the amount you HOLD the rope in your hand!

GOOD ROPE! straight and on the snow

FABULOUS ROPE TEAM

Grasshopper

rice paper

DON'T hold the rope in your hand!

Geeesh! What a buncha SLOW-POKES

№3 needs to communicate to his team!

OY!

DANGER! AWFUL ROPE management

ROPE too tight!

LAME ROPE TEAM

HUFF! PUFF!

GRAVITY!

Yawn...

GRAVITY!

ZOOM!

EEEG!

monitor your speed!

Keep all slack out of the rope!

Nº 1 scopes out the route, thinking safety first!

a.

Nº 1 speeds up while rounding corners

Nº 2 needs to back up to keep the rope snug

Nº 3 backs up too...

b.

Nº 1 now needs to slow down so Nº 2 can round the sharp corners

Nº 2 moves quick!

Nº 3 needs to back up again!

c.

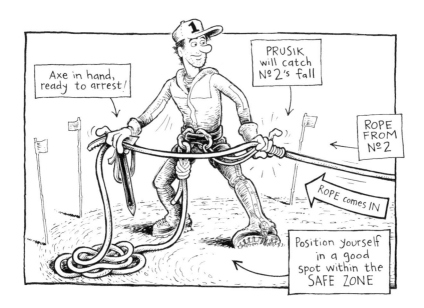

In and out of safe zones

Belaying someone into a safe zone:

1. Get a good stance or position in the safe zone.
2. Un-clip the rope from your chest harness.
3. Use one hand on the prusik; the other holds your axe and pulls the rope through the prusik.
4. Be ready to arrest if your rope mate falls into a crevasse. If there's a fall, let go of the rope (the prusik will lock) and drop into arrest position.

In particularly hazardous areas a seated hip belay is an even more secure belay technique.

To belay out of a safe zone, the same steps are followed. The rope must be let out to the leader, meaning your prusik has to be tight to your teammate before they leave the safe zone. Remember to re-clip your chest harness.

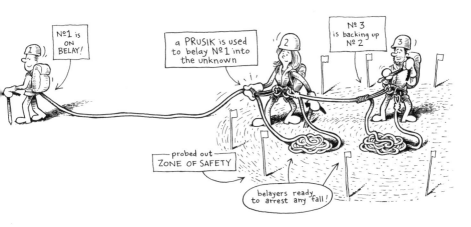

Keep the rope STRETCHED OUT for breaks during glacier travel!

There is a second method for competent parties. This is less conservative than the method above and might not be appropriate in heavily crevassed terrain.

Belaying into a safe zone (method 2):

1. The leader stops and stands in the safe zone, moving as far into the safe area as he can.

2. The 2nd and 3rd continue along the path toward the leader, they are essentially a two person team "belaying" each other with good rope management. Plus, they're traveling exactly in the leader's steps.

3. The 2nd enters the safe zone.

4. The 2nd belays the 3rd in with a prusik, following the steps above.

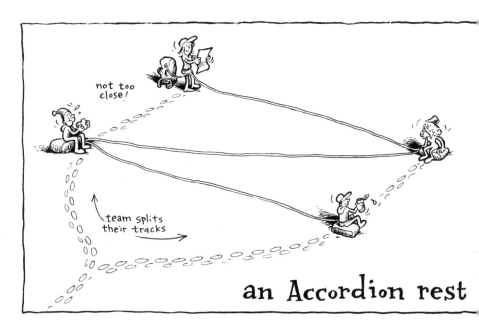

an Accordion rest

Leaving the safe zone, the first out should be attentively belayed from the far end of the zone. Then the 2nd and 3rd follow out as the rope tightens person to person.

Belaying someone in and out of a safe zone or perimeter is not a casual, nonchalant act. It's their only safety net!

Everybody walks forward in the same track, then they move to the side.

I've got chocolate!

anybody got chocolate?

well Hook me up!

DON'T GET TOO CLOSE! just enough to toss trail food to eachother

Three rope teams PARALLEL PARKING during a break

Taking breaks

Breaks are essential. On a glacier, however, it's a potential disaster to just group up — you could all fall in the same crevasse. You can easily take breaks on a stretched rope, so make sure everyone has his own food, water, and other necessities. Alternately you can rest more closely together using the "accordion" rest or, when you have multiple rope teams, the "parallel park." When you must rest in a group, gather in a safe zone, such as a rock outcrop, or snow that's been carefully probed.

The team should belay each other in and out of the safe zone, using prusiks to reel in and feed out slack. Another way to belay someone into the safe zone is to just walk to the far side of the safe zone, keeping the rope snug as your partner approaches; this requires a big zone. If the safe zone is snow, everyone should hold an ice axe and be ready to drop into self-arrest until the entire team is in. When the safe zone is ice or rock, where self-arresting is painful or impossible, it is better not to walk to the far side; instead, belay at the start/edge of the zone and stand or sit in a well-braced position.

~ SELF BELAY ~

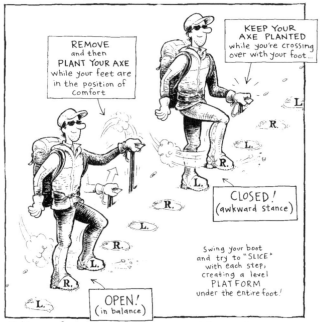

Kicking perfect steps will be appreciated by your teammates

64

MOVING, SELF-BELAY, SELF-ARREST, AND PROTECTION

ARRESTING
with
SKIS and POLES

use your
pole handle
as an
"ICE TOOL"

USE YOUR
EDGES!

The links in the chain of snow safety are: judgment, movement, self-belay, self-arrest, and finally, roped belay. Remember this order when learning or practicing techniques. Often, more time is spent focusing on self arrest and rope techniques than on self-belay or movement on snow. Stay on your feet and you won't have to test those anchors or your partner.

After judgment, your personal movement is your primary safety system. Competent mountaineers display a mastery of footwork and ice axe placement. When you travel across steep or exposed terrain, use your ice axe as a self-belay, sinking its shaft into the snow just ahead of your footsteps. The buried shaft can provide a solid support, and if you slip you can drop onto the axe and catch yourself.

Self-arrest

If you do fall, stop right away. A quick self-arrest is imperative; it is also the first step in every crevasse rescue. It is much easier to stop when you are just starting to fall than to wait until you have gained momentum. Since you never know when or how you will fall, you need to master all of the self-arrest positions including: feet first, face up; feet first, face down; head first, face down; head first, face up. Practice these positions on a smooth slope that gradually runs out into a safe, level, and obstacle-free zone. Then, practice them while you are wearing a pack. It's amazing how much more difficult a pack can make self-arresting, especially a heavy one!

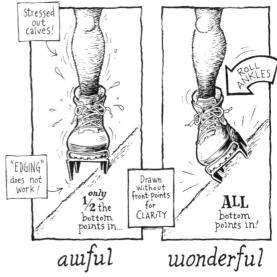

Stressed out calves!

ROLL ANKLES

"EDGING" does not work!

only 1/2 the bottom points in...

Drawn without front-points for CLARITY

ALL bottom points in!

auful   *wonderful*

Other tips: Don't trip over your crampons. Easier said than done. The key is taking short, wide steps. Flat steps are also important because these engage all of the bottom crampon points. "Edging" in crampons only uses the side points — a no-no. Be careful not to sit down or kneel; doing either can cause your crampon points to pop out of the ice.

Wearing skis or snowshoes also poses self-arrest challenges. With skis, use the metal edges and your ski pole — self-arrest-style pole grips help — to bite into the snow. Try to get most of the weight onto your ski edges. With snowshoes, self-arrest as normal, working extra hard to dig your feet in the snow. With crampons, which can catch in the snow and flip you, keep your feet off the slope and use your knees instead.

Your movement, self-belay, and self-arrest are the building blocks of glacier travel. Once you've mastered these skills you can clip into a rope team and assist others in the event of a fall. When you travel, keep the rope on your uphill side. This way if someone falls, the rope will pull you into the slope rather than spin you away from it. If a fall is likely, say you encounter a steep slope or ice step, the leader will need to protect the rope team by placing protection and clipping his rope through it. "Running protection" such as this will provide a back up to the team's self-arrests.

sharp!

Wad of DUCT TAPE, another LIFE SAVER!

alternative

USE THE BASKET END as an "ICE TOOL"

ALL THEM YEARS IN THAT OL' SADDLE...

ALWAYS WALK BOW-LEGGED when wearing CRAMPONS ON ICE

As in rock climbing, you'll encounter numerous cruxes in a crevasse field. Examples include jumping a crevasse and traversing a steep slope above a bottomless gaper. When you encounter a crux, consider if your team members will be able to self-arrest. If they can't, or you aren't sure, place a piece of solid protection and clip the rope behind you through it as a running belay, or stop, set a real belay anchor, and belay each person across, one at a time.

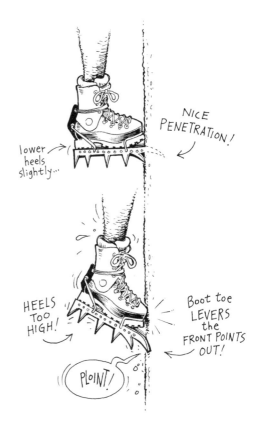

lower heels slightly...

NICE PENETRATION!

HEELS TOO HIGH!

Boot toe LEVERS the FRONT POINTS OUT!

PLOINT!

AN UPHILL FALL IS GENERALLY (But not always!) SAFER AND EASIER TO HOLD

FALLING!

Hey, this is EASY!

DIVE INTO ARREST POSITION!

IF A ROPEMATE DROPS IN, GET ANY SLACK OUT OF THE ROPE... FAST!

ROPE ACROSS DOWNHILL HIP

Holding a fall will spin you AWAY from the snow surface!

ROPE ACROSS UPHILL HIP

Holding a fall should pull you INTO arrest position toward the snow

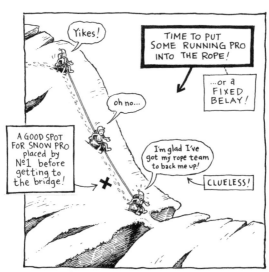

It may be impossible to expect a rope team to arrest a fall in some places!

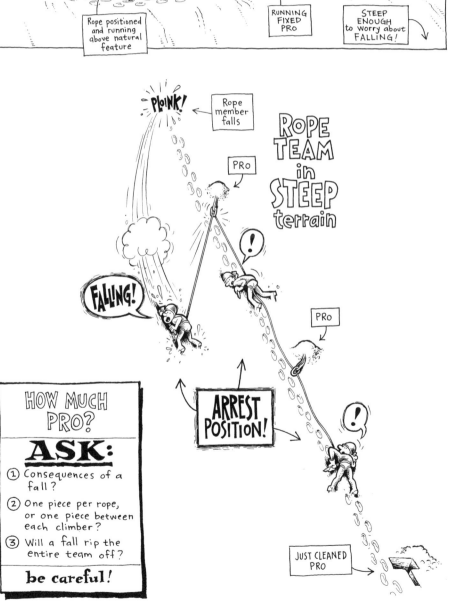

CLIPPING THRU

This technique keeps the rope clipped in
when the middle person passes the protection!

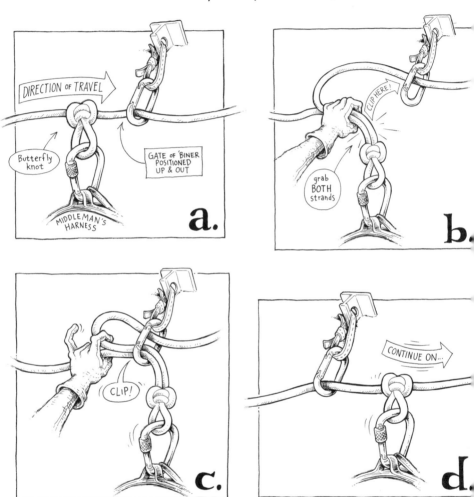

Clipping through

On a team of two, the second person will remove the point of running protection, but on teams of three or more the middle people will need to clip through the running protection, leaving it in place for the last person to clean. To clip through a point of protection without unclipping the rope and endangering the team, follow the illustrated steps above. If the point of protection has two carabiners on it, you can clip through simply by clipping the rope on the backside of your knot through one carabiner, then unclipping the rope on the front side of your knot.

**Sometimes
you've gotta
jump 'em!**

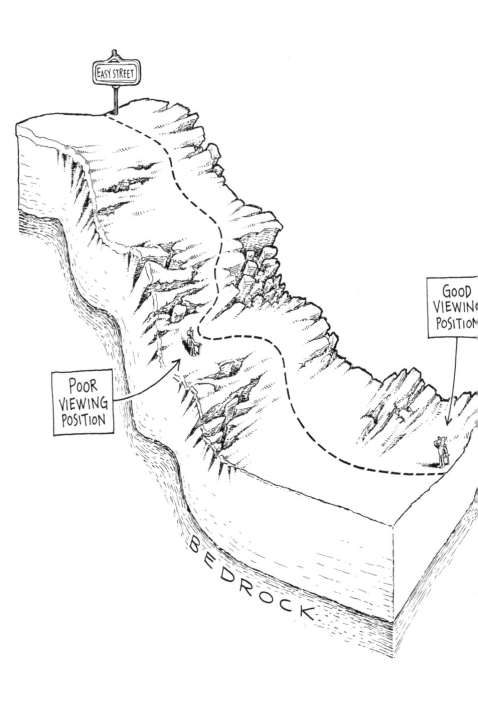

(things get interesting)

T his is the heart and soul of glacier travel. It is all about knowledge, vision, and intuition. The ideal route across a glacier will steer clear of avalanche paths, icefalls, rockfall, and seracs; if you must travel though such areas, speed and minimal exposure to the hazard are mandatory. The ideal route will also follow crevasse-free terrain with safe and easy footing. To find that path, examine the glacial surface and the topography around it.

Try to get a view of the "big picture" to see the possible crevasse areas and their general patterns. Imagine you have x-ray glasses: where would the cracks be? Look for clues on the snow surface. Look for linearities, which are long, straight crevasses that are partially or fully covered with snow. If you see an opening or a depression, you can connect the dots in a straight line and guess where the crack will be under the snow. As you cross these linearities, probe to figure out if the crack is there and how thick and strong the bridge is.

In most cases you'll see open crevasses, depressions, icefalls, seracs, and so on. One or all of these features doesn't mean "no way!" It means evaluate, and use your experience and judgment to minimize the risk. To simplify route finding, break your proposed route into sections. Visualize your line through each difficult area, using the easy, less crevassed areas to stop and regroup.

Your team's orientation to crevasses is critical. When possible, orient your team perpendicular to crevasses. This way, only one person encounters each crevasse at a time. If the route strays from perpendicular, there is the potential for a pendulum fall.

ALWAYS (or whenever possible) TRAVEL *PERPENDICULAR* to KNOWN or PROBABLE crevasses!

When perpendicular travel isn't possible, move en echelon, spaced apart and parallel to the crevasses. When the terrain prevents spreading out along the length of your rope, compress the team by echeloning in a "V" or "Z" pattern. Echelon travel of any sort can, however, be tough to coordinate since two or more people must evaluate terrain and break trail. In heavily crevassed terrain where you only have one safe route, echelon can be impractical. Here it is best to forgo echeloning and have one person route find, being extra careful with her route choices.

When you are leading, you have a responsibility to the entire team. You need to set a good pace breaking trail, probe when necessary, and communicate with the rest of the team, who might offer good advice about the route.

The vantage point of the second person, for example, often allows him to see obstacles or potential hazards that are out of sight to the leader. The second can also help the leader by speeding up or slowing down to keep slack out of the rope.

Echelon travel

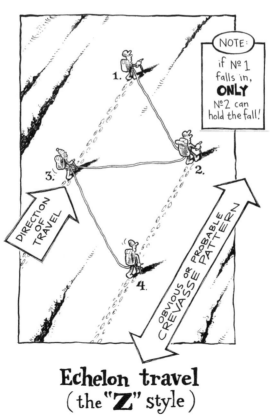

Echelon travel
(the "Z" style)

75

THE PROBLEMATIC ROLE OF THE
MISUNDERSTOOD MIDDLEMAN

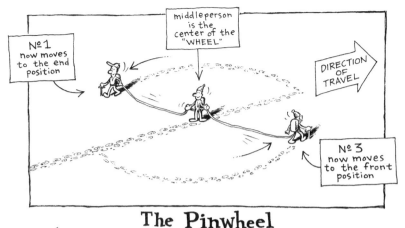

No 1
now moves
to the end
position

middleperson
is the
center of the
"WHEEL"

DIRECTION
OF
TRAVEL

No 3
now moves
to the front
position

The Pinwheel
(this is more complicated with a four person rope team)

The last person on the rope is in a mellow spot, but he must pay attention and be prepared to self-arrest at any moment. The leader could dead end, and the easiest way to proceed might be to turn around and have the caboose take over as leader. Better know where to go!

Even if you don't need to backtrack, you'll usually need to alternate leading. On a rope of two the easiest way to change leaders is to trade positions while you are both in a safe zone. When you have three people on a rope, you can use the "pinwheel" method: the middle person stops while the leader and third person revolve around him until the leader and third person have reversed positions.

Pinwheeling won't be possible when your path is too narrow to spread out an entire rope's width. Then you can change leaders using the "inchworm" technique as shown.

No 3
keeps
walking

No 2
STops

No 1
STops

←belaying

a.

belaying

No 3 is
Now out front
as No 1!

b.

No 3 KEEPS WALKING PAST No 2

belaying

Once the rope is
fully out,
all travel as usual!

c.

Inchworm

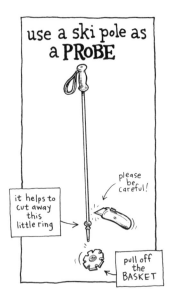

use a ski pole as a **PROBE**

it helps to cut away this little ring →

please be careful!

← pull off the BASKET

an old SKI POLE with the basket removed is an excellent alternative to an axe or a full on avalanche probe

an ICE AXE usually too short **&** too thick t be an effect PROBE

Probing: why, when, how, and where

You're leading and suspect hidden hazards. Time to pull out the probe and find out for sure. Do so by holding your probe vertically — an ice axe works in a pinch, but a ski pole with basket removed works better if you don't have a real probe — and sliding or punching it down into the snow in front of you. The resistance you feel through the probe will indicate what is underneath. If you feel consistent resistance, move forward and probe again. If you feel no resistance — obvious air! — you've hit a crevasse.

Can the snow cover support your weight and then the weight of your ropemates? This depends on the snowpack and conditions. You can get a feel for the strength of the snow by stomping on the solid snow under-foot. How far do you punch in, how soft or hard is the snow, and how does this snow compare to the snow over the crevasse?

Whatever you discover, tell everyone about it. If there is a hazard, draw a line in the snow just in front of it and

GOOD PROBING Technique!

keep cord tie-o

DANGEROUS PROBING Technique!

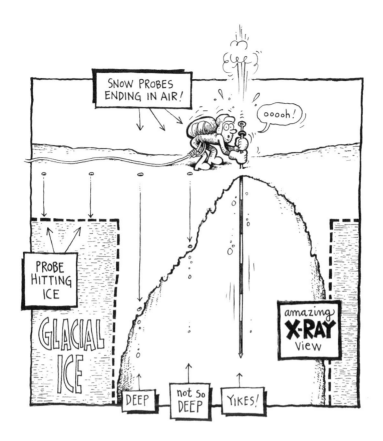

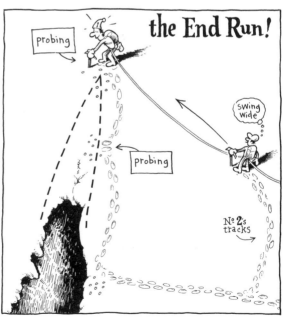

tell everyone to tread past the line with extreme caution. Drawing an "X" in the snow means. "Don't step here!" Crossed wands are also good for marking crevasses; they don't get erased like marks in the snow.

If you are following on a rope, take care to step exactly in the footprints of your leader. Pay attention: you can easily mistake rope-drag and axe marks as footprints — and step right into a hidden crevasse.

Whiteout navigation

Traveling in a whiteout is not recommended, though it is inevitable in the life of a mountaineer. A common example: You leave camp on a clear summit day, but on your way back to camp you are in a full whiteout with blowing snow that has obliterated your path. You would have marked your path with wands, but you chose not to bring them because weather conditions looked great in the morning.

Wands are four-foot long sticks (usually bamboo tomato stakes, though willow branches or sticks will work) with a piece of ribbon or a duct-tape "flag" attached to the top. Stick these along the route and you can retrace your steps, even if they've melted out or are under new snow.

The distance between wands varies, but it is common to place one every ropelength, or every 50 meters (32 wands to a mile). Figuring out this spacing is simple. The leader simply places a wand and moves on. When the last person on the rope arrives at that wand he yells "wand!" The leader, hearing this, then places another wand.

To retrace a wanded route, have the last person on a rope stand by a wand while the leader swings out in an arc. The next wand will lie at a point along this arc.

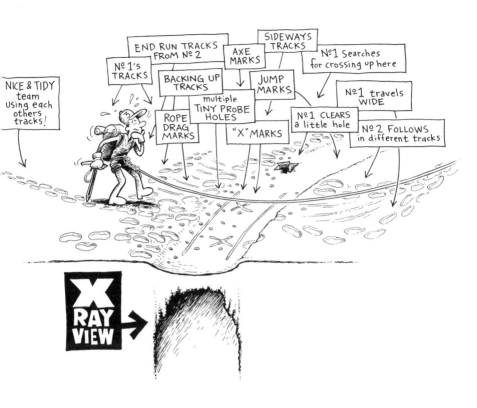

NICE & TIDY team using each others tracks!

N°1's TRACKS

END RUN TRACKS FROM N°2

BACKING UP TRACKS

multiple TINY PROBE HOLES

ROPE DRAG MARKS

AXE MARKS

SIDEWAYS TRACKS

"X" MARKS

JUMP MARKS

N°1 Searches for crossing up here

N°1 travels WIDE

N°1 CLEARS a little hole

N°2 FOLLOWS in different tracks

You can place intermediate wands to mark important turns through crevasse fields, or crevasses to step over. Avoid placing them in low valleys and depressions where they can't be seen. Do place them on highly visible hill crests.

Wands save lives, and thwart emergency bivies. They are cheap insurance!

The perimeter of a probed safe zone, like camp, needs to be wanded. There are other uses for wands like using them to make wand "fences" to catch or funnel you back to camp or to a cache. For a fence, anticipate the direction you will return from and wand perpendicular to this in either direction.

Painted bamboo does not grow on glaciers; therefore wands are trash and should be removed. The exception is wands you find on a high traffic trade route like Disappointment Cleaver on Mount Rainier. Take yours home but leave the ones already in place.

DARK colored DUCT TAPE "FLAG"

about 4 FEET tall!

8 to 12 inches below snow

POINTY END

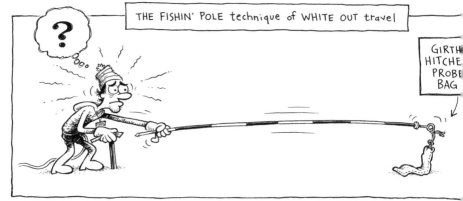

an alternate use for the avalanche probe!
(what's up? what's down?)

A savvy glacier traveler wands her route when she suspects trouble on the return trip. She also carries a map and compass and knows how to use them. Map and compass navigation are beyond the scope of this book, but here are a few pointers.

First, the metal in your ice axe can deflect the magnetic compass needle. Prevent this by holding compass and ice axe in different hands.

Second, your body has a tendency to turn to one side while your compass points to where you actually want to go. Your cockeyed body position causes

Whiteout Travel!
(bizarreness...)

you to veer off course. Correct this by concentrating on walking in a straight line. Better, have the last person in your team carry the compass and sight down the rope or line of heads and call out directions to place the leader on track. The leader then marks an X in the snow to the side of the trail and everyone advances until the person with the compass arrives at the X. The compass guy then sights back down the rope, readjusts the leader, and so on. This method uses the roped team as a constant direction of travel arrow, and is very effective for holding a straight path, though time consuming.

In some cases the light and terrain are so disorienting that using something like the fishin' pole pictured on page 82 can help you figure out what is actually in front of you: crevasses, a drop off, going up, going down, all sorts of good information! Laugh now, once in this situation it will all make sense!

You can supplement and expedite your map and compass work with visual aids, such as "hand rails," or natural features like a ridge, cliff band, slope, drop-off, moraine, or anything that you can walk into and identify with little visibility. Link a series of hand rails like dots on a map and you can go where you need to go.

GPS (Global Positioning System) is a great tool on big glaciers and ice-fields. Recording "waypoints" for camps, caches, and routes is easy and accurate with these super-small and accurate tools. They are no substitute for proficiency with map and compass, though they certainly have their place as an emergency aid.

White-out truths revealed

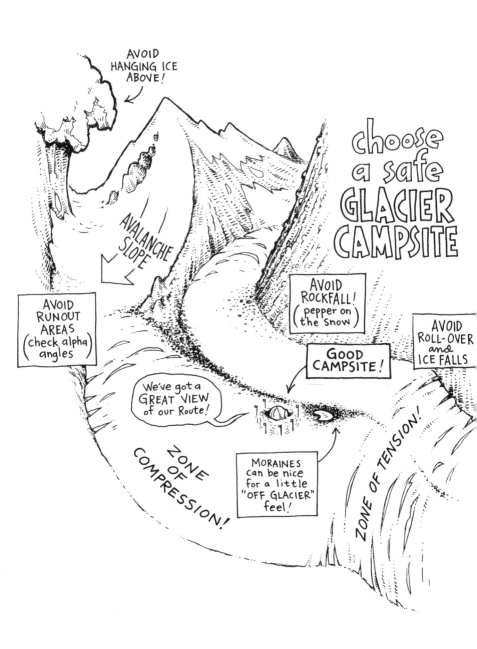

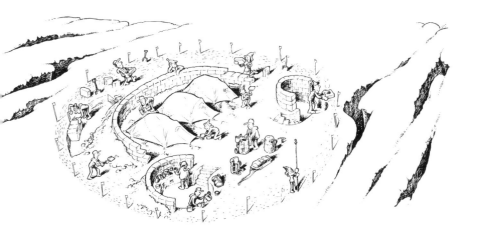

A well-selected and constructed glacier camp is a wonderful place, a safe and cozy haven tucked among the hazards that have been gnawing at you all day. A badly selected or built camp, on the other hand, is a constant worry: Did you pitch camp over a crevasse that might swallow you at any moment? Is that snow slope overhead so close it can bury you if it slides?

Proper site selection and preparation will stack the odds in favor of a comfortable glacier camp.

Site selection

On small glaciers, your best camp might be off the glacier, over in the crevasse-free dry ground of dirt and stone. On large glaciers you'll have to set up camp on the ice. Your first concern should be whether your proposed camp is in a potential avalanche run-out zone. Slopes with angles of between 30 to 45 degrees are the most likely to avalanche. Locate your camp keeping in mind the "Alpha Angle," which tells you the probable distance an avalanche will run.

Identify any slopes that might slide, and measure the angle from where you are to the top of the suspect slope. This "alpha" should be less than 21 degrees in a melt-freeze snowpack, less than 17 degrees in a soft-cold snowpack.

The melt-freeze snowpack can be stable in the summer. During winter storms and early in the spring, however, it can be very dangerous. When it slides it is usually the new snow layer that breaks loose during the day after a storm — but not always. In the spring, large snow slopes can slide off the rock slabs they are sitting on. A slide of this sort is a "full-depth" avalanche, extremely powerful and deadly. In late spring, large, wet-snow avalanches can occur when the snowpack becomes saturated with water due to warming temperatures.

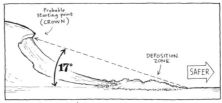

ALPHA ANGLES:

Probable starting point (CROWN)

17°

DEPOSITION ZONE

SAFER

SOFT / COLD SNOWPACK

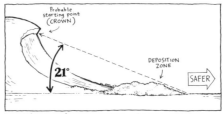

Probable starting point (CROWN)

21°

DEPOSITION ZONE

SAFER

MELT / FREEZE SNOWPACK

(Camp and travel beyond the ALPHA ANGLE in avalanche terrain)

A soft, cold snowpack has persistent weak layers that are caused by low temperatures throughout the year. In this snowpack, natural-release avalanches usually happen during, and the day after, a storm. Human-triggered avalanches may occur many days later, since instabilities persist. Soft, cold snowpacks have the potential to be weak at the base, producing full-depth avalanches throughout the year.

Avalanches are an important subject for all glacier travelers and mountaineers. This book only briefly touches on the subject, on which many excellent books are written. For a more detailed yet concise study, read *Snow Sense*, by Doug Fesler and Jill Fredston.

Ice avalanches — from icefalls and seracs — can occur any time, regardless of angle or temperature. Ice avalanches are unpredictable and can run extremely long distances, even across low-angle terrain. Beware, and set camp well away from any icefall or serac hazard.

Although you are on a glacier, consider rockfall. A nearby cliff or moraine wall could pose a

Don't just focus on what's under your feet, dangers lurk above too!

16 TONS

GOLLY! a big block of ICE!

LET'S BOOGIE!

threat, rolling boulders or dumping walls of dirt and debris across the glacier. The edges of glaciers and medial moraines tend to be high rock-fall zones. Be especially wary when recent rain or snowmelt has saturated the ground around the glacier.

Probing a safe area

You have found a nice spot well away from rockfall, icefall, and avalanches. Time to pull out the probe and determine if there are any crevasses lurking about. Ideally you want to know beyond a shadow of doubt that you are camping on solid snow and ice. Unfortunately, you'll seldom know for certain, but thorough probing will usually tell you when there's enough snow underfoot to support your camp. Use your knowledge of glacier anatomy and pick a zone of compression.

Probing in a circle yields a nice camp area. To do this, have the middle person stand still while the end members prusik in on the rope, stopping at a distance that will equal the campsite diameter. Next, the middle person belays the end members while they probe every couple of feet, making a circle.

After the initial circle, the end people probe the middle of the circle. Continue probing until everyone agrees the site is crevasse-free or has a considerable base of snow underfoot. Once this is decided, you can declare the site safe, belay everyone in, unrope, and wand the perimeter. Wand the circle a bit smaller than what was probed, just for that extra buffer.

Site preparation

Wind and snowfall are your glacier camp's worst enemies. A glacier's extreme temperature variations create wind regardless of what the rest of the atmosphere is doing. A glacier's micro

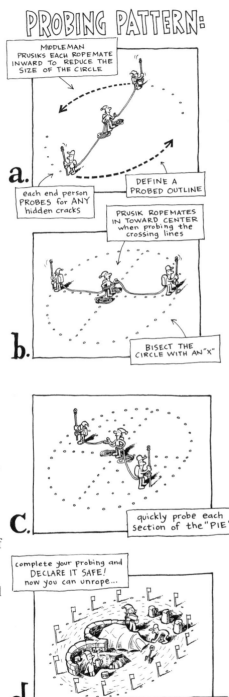

PROBING PATTERN:

a. MIDDLE MAN PRUSIKS EACH ROPEMATE INWARD TO REDUCE THE SIZE OF THE CIRCLE

each end person PROBES for ANY hidden cracks

DEFINE A PROBED OUTLINE

b. PRUSIK ROPEMATES IN TOWARD CENTER when probing the crossing lines

BISECT THE CIRCLE WITH AN "X"

c. quickly probe each section of the "PIE"

complete your probing and DECLARE IT SAFE! now you can unrope...

d. WAND the PERIMETER of the safe zone

climate can produce powerful down glacier (katabatic) winds or up glacier (adiabatic) winds, depending on the time of day. These winds can be devastating. Wind walls for tents are key. Snow shelters are even better.

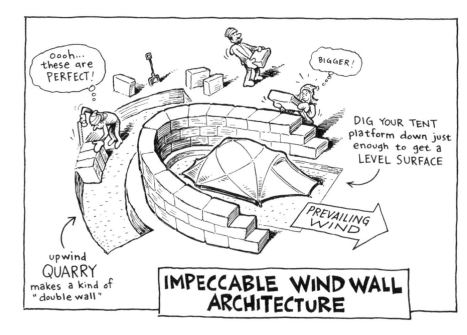

Thoughts on wind walls:

1. The thicker the wall, the stronger the wall. Thin walls can blow down, or quickly melt in sunshine. Build your walls as thick as you can. One and a half to two feet thick is good, especially if there are few or no holes between the snow blocks.

2. Build the wall at least as high as the tent, shielding it from the prevailing wind direction. If you aren't certain where the wind will come from, encircle your tent area with a wall.

3. Build the walls so there is enough room to shovel between the walls and the tent, but not so much room that the wall is too far away to do any good. Two to four feet from tent to snow wall should suffice.

4. Pitch the tent with its door and cooking vestibule facing away from the wind.

5. Keep shovels handy for emergency storm work.

6. Keep gear organized so it doesn't get buried or blown away.

7. If you are in a really exposed camp, build a snow shelter such as an igloo or snow cave and don't even set up the tent.

Camp comfort

Being prepared for wind and snow is mandatory. Beyond that, comfort is the name of the game.

PITIFUL WIND WALLS!

good blocks

WIND WALL
architecture

Andy

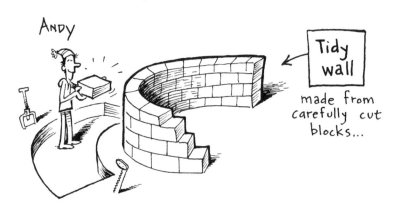

Tidy wall

made from carefully cut blocks...

Mike

SLOPPY WALL

made from clumps of snow tossed in a pile!

MOUND UP SNOW!

Both TIDY & SLOPPY WALLS WILL REQUIRE **BOLSTERING** as a REINFORCEMEN AGAINST WIND & SUN!

and thus, the trip endeth...

First up is a snow kitchen. Digging out the floor of your tent vestibule makes the simplest kitchen. Watch for stove fumes and fires; people have died from these mundane hazards. A more elaborate snow kitchen is a pit dug in the snow, near your tent. A nice, deep kitchen with benches carved into the wall works well for getting out of the wind and provides a comfortable cooking and living area. As you dig the kitchen, use the removed snow blocks to build surrounding wind walls. In a cushy snow kitchen, the outside wall is as high as the chef's head, and there's a sheltered counter space to cook on. In a storm this kitchen will fill in with snow, so keep the stuff in it organized.

Sunny weather or wind can erode your site, so be prepared to maintain it. This will include tightening your tent's guy lines, restaking the anchors, and moving your tent as the snow under and around it melts.

Water

If the sun is cranking, use it to your advantage and build a solar still to melt snow or ice for drinking water.

ooooh!

APPENDIX

removable BLADE

GENERAL ICE AXE

When using a mountaineering SHOVEL BLADE on an ICE TOOL REMEMBER... Always point the pick AWAY FROM YOURSELF! (and tents too)

Be prepared to maintain your tent platform over time!

minimal head room

and

SUN BAKED TENT PLATFORM!

TENT DEADMEN melted out!

consider AVALANCHE danger!

vent hole(s)

drawn without heat trap

Z

dome shaped interior

KEEP A SHOVEL inside

front porch

heat trap

THROW SNOW DOWNHILL

[amazing X-RAY view]

SNOW CAVE

assistant

chef!

VENT OPEN!

VENT OPEN!

(attempt) ORGANIZATION

sleeping bags, down coats (etc) in a big GARBAGE BAG

If you're too lazy to build a snow kitchen, or if it's stormy, the vestibule is a cramped alternative — but be careful!

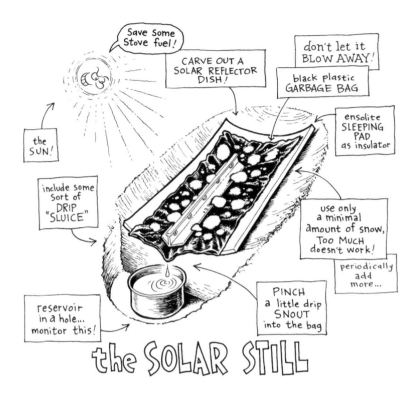

the SOLAR STILL

A simple still can provide all of your camp's water needs, saving stove fuel. The above illustration shows it all.

Leave no trace

One of the basic tenets of visiting a wild place is leaving it wild for the next person. In any situation it is easy to get complacent toward the environment, but it's especially easy to slack off on a glacier, where things disappear into the snow, down a crevasse, down a wall, or over a cliff. Laziness and complacency are unacceptable. Plan ahead and prepare your expedition to practice clean, eco-groovy camping. The following are the basic Leave No Trace (LNT) principals, followed by thoughts on that one waste we don't want to bring home.

Eco-groovy L.N.T. principles
1. Plan ahead and prepare.
2. Travel and camp on durable surfaces.
3. Properly dispose of wastes.
4. Leave what you find.
5. Minimize campfire impacts.
6. Respect wildlife.
7. Be considerate of other visitors.

Pooping

"Dumping" poses disposal challenges, though there are environmentally acceptable methods for disposing of your feces. Problems arise on the glacier. A cat hole in the snow is NOT acceptable, especially in popular areas. As the season wears on, snow melts. Feces lying on the surface, with brown stained snow ringing them, are obvious evidence of an ignorant and lazy traveler. It's a nasty sight, though common on popular routes.

Contaminated surface snow may be unsightly, but it's also unsanitary, leaching toxins into the general snowpack. When it is time for you to gather snow to melt for water, it's a challenge finding clean snow.

One partial solution is to dig latrines. These can work if they are super deep and are used by everyone (such as the 20-foot-deep latrine at the 14,200-foot camp on Denali). But, if a latrine is shallow it is just a larger waste dump waiting to melt out and expose its foul load.

A better solution for big and cold glaciers is to get your dump in a crevasse. A nice, friendly crevasse with solid sides and a smooth, narrow opening is perfect for a low-impact latrine. Use a shovel to dig away the loose snow and ice around the crevasse, making a sturdy and safe latrine for groggy morning excursions.

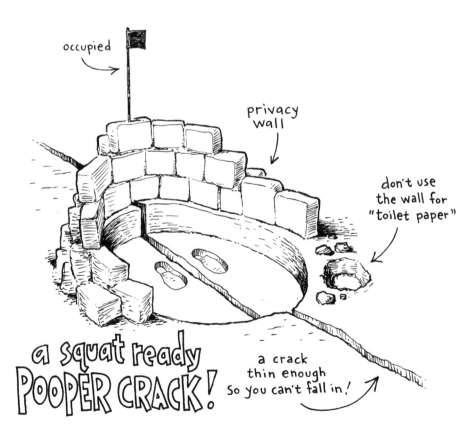

occupied

privacy wall

don't use the wall for "toilet paper"

a squat ready POOPER CRACK!

a crack thin enough so you can't fall in!

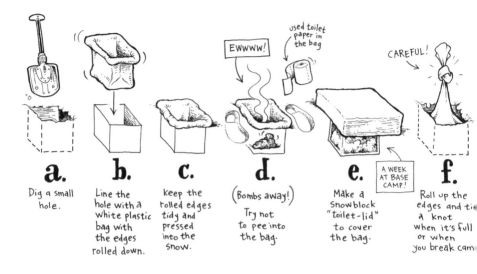

a.
Dig a small hole.

b.
Line the hole with a white plastic bag with the edges rolled down.

c.
keep the rolled edges tidy and pressed into the snow.

d.
(Bombs away!)
Try not to pee into the bag.

EWWWW!

used toilet paper in the bag

e.
Make a snow block "toilet-lid" to cover the bag.

A WEEK AT BASE CAMP!

CAREFUL!

f.
Roll up the edges and ti[e] a knot when it's full or when you break cam[p]

Unfortunately, the perfect straddle crevasse doesn't always present itself. So, another effective method is to dump on a hunk of packed snow, and toss it into a gaper. This method also lets you use a wide crevasse, and is a good alternative for people who are nervous about straddling icy doom. For comfort and privacy, you may want to build a latrine fort, such as the one illustrated.

At any glacier latrine, you can use snow to wipe, which is the best, low-impact option. If you do use toilet paper, carry it out in a plastic trash bag. You might also try a wipe or two with snow, followed by one with TP.

The next option is a plastic-bag latrine. You can usually use a plastic bag for a number of days, then toss it in a deep crevasse. This method adds a trash bag to your organic waste, but is better than contaminating the surface snow. Further, by the time the bag shows up at the snout of the glacier it probably will be tough to recognize — glaciers crush boulders into dust. This isn't a

the **BAG**

for tossing into an open crevasse!

perfect solution; you're dumping poop and trash directly into the environment. Someday there may be a better way.

Finally, you may need to carry out all feces. This is required on some mountains, such as Mount Rainier, Mount Hood, and some places on Denali. Even when carrying out your feces isn't a law you may want to do it anyway. On warm, small glaciers such as those in the North Cascades or Swiss Alps, feces in a crevasse can quickly enter the area's water system. Both the North Cascades and Swiss Alps are heavily used — that means lots of dumps right in the rivers. Yuck.

What about pee?

Urine isn't much of a health concern; eating yellow snow generally won't hurt you. Nonetheless, urine-contaminated snow is unsightly, smells, and is nasty. Designate a pee spot away from your drinking-water-snow quarry, and have everyone go there. Don't pee in your plastic bag latrine, or you'll have a real problem when a hole develops.

Ravens

These birds, common on glaciers, are regarded as a good omen by many native people, but are cursed by mountaineers for stealing food and wreaking havoc on caches. Ravens are naturally inquisitive, especially about caches and unattended camps. I've had to clean up after a raven strike: food bits and trash are everywhere, friendly and (now habituated) ravens are probably sick, and you

cache etiquette

will be on tight rations for the rest of the trip. Respect the ways of the wild, and take the time to camp clean. Keep the tent zippers closed in unattended camps and maintain neat kitchen areas. Cover your food cache with snow or rocks, marking it with wands taped together in case of a deep snow.

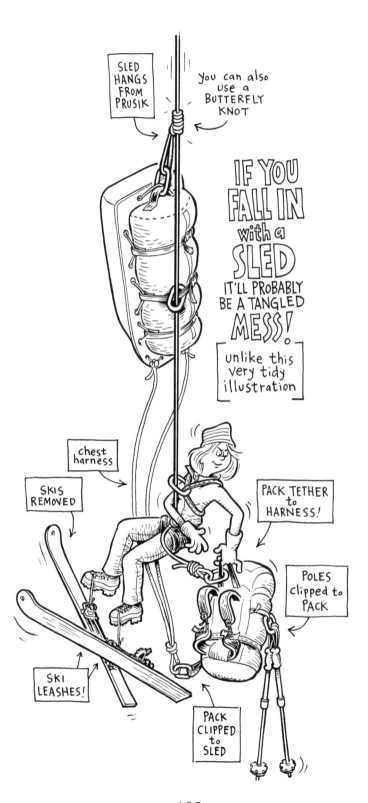

The unavoidable has happened — you or one of your teammates has fallen into a crevasse. In some cases, the crevasse fall is minor, say, up to the knees or waist, and doesn't weight the rope. Then, extraction is as easy as having the team keep the rope taut or gently tug on it to aid their stricken teammate out of the slot. This is a "punch through," as in: "Wow, the snow really softened up on the way down today — I punched through three times."

Things get more complicated when someone falls completely — over their head — into a
crevasse. Then, you immediately put five steps to work:

1. **Arrest the fall**
2. **Build an anchor**
3. **Check on the victim**
4. **Rescue***
5. **Regroup**

* You can further break Step 4 into four options: climbing, prusiking, lowering, and hauling. Allowing the victim to get out under his own power is ideal; using a haul system is the most elaborate and time-consuming. Always go for the easiest option. Don't dive into the most complex solution just because you've learned and practiced it.

These five steps can be accomplished in multiple ways and everyone has variations, tricks, and "better" systems. Develop and use your favorite methods. Regardless of what you ultimately use, make sure:

1. The system is backed up. Don't end up with one piece of 6mm perlon or a sketchy ice-axe plant holding the victim. Use gear that's overkill for the task and double it up if there's any doubt.

2. Everyone in your team knows the same or a similar system. Setting up a rescue system requires teamwork — difficult if everyone is operating on different pages.

3. Keep it simple. Gidgets, gadgets, and doodads get lost, dropped, or just don't work. Learn a system that performs well with little gear and can be improvised from common items such as carabiners, slings, and prusiks.

All the complicated rescue systems are meant to be practiced. These skills can only be learned by doing. Hands-on experience is the best way to integrate these systems into your brain. If all you've done is just read this book, it won't be enough when you have to deal with a real-life emergency.

Prusiking, climbing out, and lowering
In most cases rigging a haul system is unnecessary, and it's faster, simpler, and safer to have the person in the crevasse climb or prusik out, or lower to the bottom of the crevasse and traverse up and out.

(almost)
Impossible to climb out

Easy to climb out

STEMMING may be a SIMPLE SOLUTION rather than creating a complex rescue

Climbing out. If the victim is able and the crevasse walls look climbable, climbing out is a simple method of extraction. When climbing is reasonable, the person or persons on the surface should rig an equalized anchor and belay the victim out of the hole.

Prusiking. Prusiking is a quick and easy way for the victim to get himself out of a crevasse. As always in any crevasse extraction, anchor the rope to two equalized pieces. Beyond that, all the victim needs is encouragement and some help getting himself and pack over the crevasse lip. The illustrations show how even a small overhanging lip can pose challenges.

If the lip is nasty, the victim may need to transfer his prusiks to another rope that is set over a well-prepared spot, one that has been cleared of loose snow. But, before the victim climbs out on this second rope he needs to help haul out his pack, or it, too, could get jammed under the crevasse lip. Alternately, the victim could clip his pack to the second rope for later retrieval (see page 107).

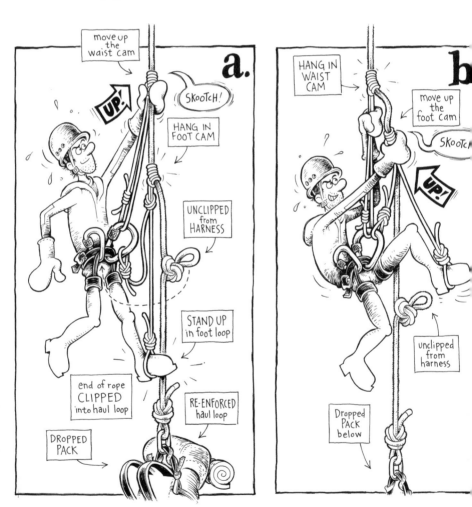

Fixed rope ascension with two prusiks!

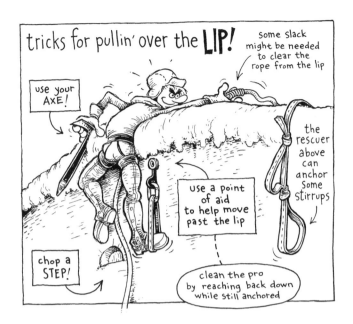

Lowering. Crevasses are sometimes filled in with snow or ice blocks, creating a floor, or might just be shallow. In these situations the victim might be able to just walk out of the crevasse. CAUTION: A crevasse can have a false bottom — never allow the victim to untie or go off belay.

If lowering and walking out is reasonable, the climbers on top rig the rope exactly as they would for a haul, but use a Munter hitch on the rope at the master-point tie-off rather than a figure eight. They then release the Munter/Mule that holds the ratchet prusik, allowing the Munter hitch at the master point to take the weight. The last step is to remove the ratchet prusik and lower the victim, who then hikes out, belayed from above via the Munter hitch.

Sometimes
y'can just walk
out of a crevasse!

Three-person rescue

If the victim can climb, prusik, or walk out of the crevasse, all the better. Hauling the victim out requires much more time and energy, but is required when he is injured or incapacitated. A thorough understanding of the knots covered in Chapter 2 and the hauling systems explained in Chapter 8 is essential to a timely and efficient rescue.

In this book, we'll concentrate on a scenario where one member of a three-person team falls into a crevasse. We do this because the basics that we use for a three-person rope rescue are similar to those you'd use on any rescue. Learn the three-person rescue and you can deal with most any situation. With practice, it should take a team of beginners about 30 minutes to complete the following rescue sequence. Here goes:

1 Larry unexpectedly falls in a crevasse. He yells "Falling!" to alert the other team members.

Moe, the middle man, yells "Arrest!", dives backward to take slack out of the rope, and drops into self-arrest. Curly, who is bringing up the rear, also runs back to pull his section of rope taut, and self-arrests.

Larry has arrived at the end of his fall. Since he forgot to wear a chest harness, his heavy pack has flipped him upside down and tweaked his back.

Middle-man Moe's big job, now that he has successfully arrested the fall, is to make sure he is fully holding Larry's weight. He should get solid footing and get as comfortable as possible, since he will be in arrest position for awhile. When he is certain he is holding all of Larry's weight, he communicates to Curly.

Curly then tells Moe that he's coming up to help. He uses his prusik to self-belay along the rope to Moe, being careful to watch for cracks in the area. He assesses the scene and if prudent probes around Moe to make sure the rescue staging area is free of crevasses. He can then drop his pack near Moe and get to work building an anchor.

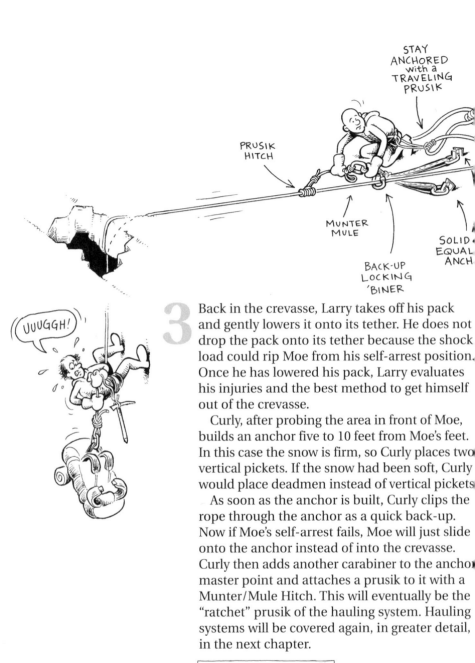

STAY ANCHORED with a TRAVELING PRUSIK

PRUSIK HITCH

MUNTER MULE

BACK-UP LOCKING 'BINER

SOLID EQUAL ANCH

UUUGGH!

Back in the crevasse, Larry takes off his pack and gently lowers it onto its tether. He does not drop the pack onto its tether because the shock load could rip Moe from his self-arrest position. Once he has lowered his pack, Larry evaluates his injuries and the best method to get himself out of the crevasse.

Curly, after probing the area in front of Moe, builds an anchor five to 10 feet from Moe's feet. In this case the snow is firm, so Curly places two vertical pickets. If the snow had been soft, Curly would place deadmen instead of vertical pickets.

As soon as the anchor is built, Curly clips the rope through the anchor as a quick back-up. Now if Moe's self-arrest fails, Moe will just slide onto the anchor instead of into the crevasse. Curly then adds another carabiner to the anchor master point and attaches a prusik to it with a Munter/Mule Hitch. This will eventually be the "ratchet" prusik of the hauling system. Hauling systems will be covered again, in greater detail, in the next chapter.

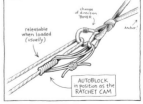

change of direction 'biner

Anchor!

releasable when loaded (usually)

AUTOBLOCK in position as the RATCHET CAM

CURLEY'S PACK

MOE IS THE ONLY ANCHOR FOR LARRY & CURLEY! (until the rope is attached to the anchor)

OK... You can ease up now and let Larry's weight transfer to the anchor!

STAY ANCHORED!

MOE STAYS READY TO ARREST if the anchor FAILS

THE ANCHOR NOW HAS ALL of LARRY'S weight

MUNTER MULE KNOT is now load bearing

LOCKER! (as BACK-UP)

SINK YOUR TOOL and CLIP IT TO THE ROPE

back ds to thin CH

WARM LAYERS need to be easy to get at

4 Larry in the crevasse has discovered that his injured back will prevent him from climbing out on his own. Finding the bowels of the glacier frosty, and figuring snow will get knocked on him during the haul to topside, he puts on his warm clothing, including a cap and gloves or mitts, which he'll need when he scrambles over the snowy crevasse lip.

Back on top of the glacier, Curly pulls all of the slack out of his belay prusik and tells Moe that Moe can slowly ease up and allow Larry's weight to transfer onto the anchor. As Moe lets the weight come onto the anchor, Curly monitors the anchor and system to make sure it is holding.

In this example Larry is only slightly injured and does not require immediate medical assistance. If he were badly hurt or unconscious, Curly would grab the first-aid kit, immediately rappel to him, and administer first aid (See page 128).

The anchor holds. Moe takes off his pack, which he sets out of the way next to Curly's pack.

Curly next creeps toward the crevasse, using his prusik as a belay. As he nears the crevasse, he probes in front of him and calls to Larry, who tells him the extent of his injuries and describes the crevasse. Larry tells Curly that the lip of the crevasse overhangs one foot. Curly now knows that he must stay at least one foot away from the edge of the crevasse.

Moe now ties a figure eight on a bight in the rope just behind the back-up carabiner, and clips this knot to the anchor.

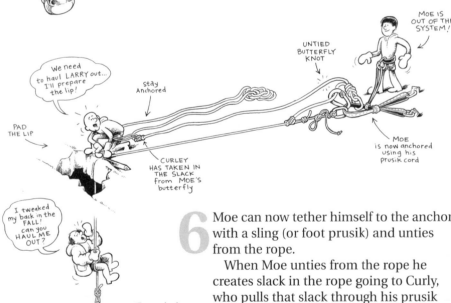

Moe can now tether himself to the anchor with a sling (or foot prusik) and unties from the rope.

When Moe unties from the rope he creates slack in the rope going to Curly, who pulls that slack through his prusik to keep the rope taut.

Once Curly gets close enough, he pads the crevasse lip with his ice-axe shaft in anticipation of hauling out Larry.

CLIP ROPE into the PULLEY 'BINER

YOUR ANCHOR PRUSIK is on the top of the "Z"

stay anchored

MOE is ready to UNCLIP and UNTIE the figure 8 on a bight

HAULING prusik

7 Curly then attaches a prusik and carabiner to the rope as a pulley point. He clips the rope coming from the anchor into the pulley carabiner and asks Moe to untie the figure-eight knot at the anchor.

Moe unties the figure eight while keeping the rope clipped through the master point.

Curly clips the unweighted side of the rope to the pulley carabiner and starts hauling.

1-2-3 HAAAAUL!

MOE tends the

8 As Curly hauls, Larry gives a hand by pulling up on his ice axe. Moe tends the ratchet prusik, making sure that it doesn't slide up and through the master-point carabiner.

LARRY may be able to help the UPWARD PROGRESS (even if only a little)

the FULLBACK

the CRAB!

HAULING TECHNIQUES

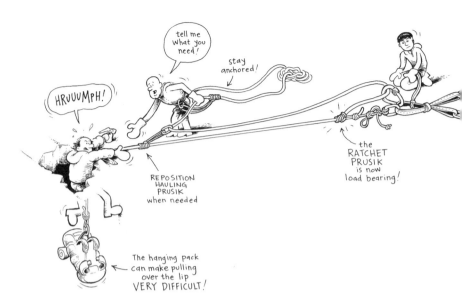

9   Even with an ice axe padding the crevasse lip, the weighted haul rope has cut into the snow, making it hard for Larry to clear the lip. He tells Curly this. Curly stops hauling and goes forward to help Larry get over the lip. By moving forward, Curly causes the hauling prusik to unweight and the ratchet prusik to take the load. Curly can reposition the hauling prusik if he has to haul again. If Larry needs to be lowered because he is getting crushed at the lip, it is Moe's job to safely reverse the system.

  He's in luck, because the system is built to reverse at the ratchet prusik. All that's necessary is for Curly to slack off his haul, causing the ratchet prusik to load. Moe would then release the mule hitch, and lower Larry on the Munter hitch. (Careful! Curly is the back up, so be attentive.) If Larry needed to be lowered farther than the length of the lowering cord, Moe would place a belay device or tie a Munter hitch in the rope at the anchor, and let the weight transfer onto this

10   The last step. The Stooges regroup at the anchor. They relax and discuss what to do next. They redivide the rope and reset their travel system.

Advanced technique:

For experienced teams in reasonable conditions, there is a faster way to check on the fallen climber and build the anchor. Provided the snow is solid, place a single anchor and use the anchor-building team member as a back up, as illustrated. If prudent, Moe can place a second picket (and be ready to jump into self arrest if necessary) while Curly checks on Larry.

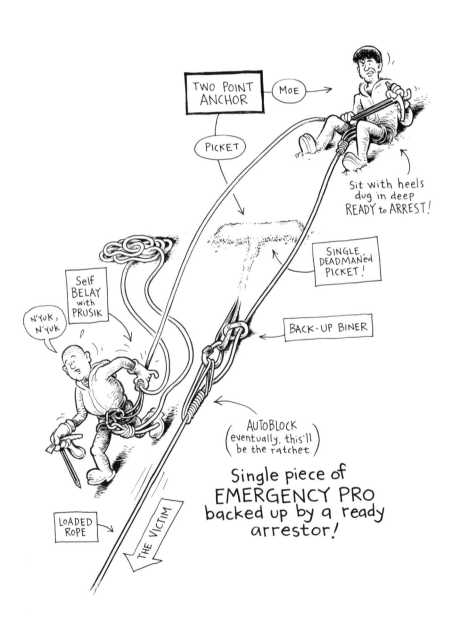

TWO POINT ANCHOR — MOE →

PICKET

Sit with heels dug in deep READY to ARREST!

SINGLE DEADMANed PICKET!

Self BELAY with PRUSIK

N'YUK, N'YUK

BACK-UP BINER

AUTOBLOCK (eventually, this'll be the ratchet)

Single piece of EMERGENCY PRO backed up by a ready arrestor!

LOADED ROPE

THE VICTIM

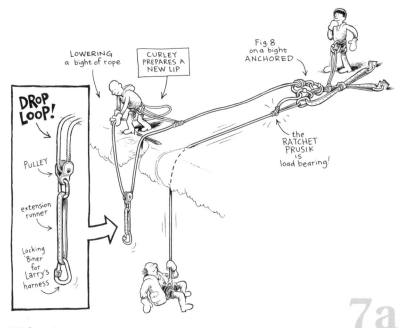

LOWERING a bight of rope

CURLEY PREPARES A NEW LIP

Fig. 8 on a bight ANCHORED

DROP LOOP!

PULLEY

extension runner

Locking 'Biner for Larry's harness

the RATCHET PRUSIK IS load bearing!

7a

The "C drop"

If Larry's rope has cut deeply into an overhanging crevasse lip, it may be necessary to prepare a different lip over which to haul him out. The C drop is a fast, efficient rescue system in this instance. The C drop may also be used if you desire an extra level of redundancy. This system backs up the victim's (Larry's) rope.

To build a C drop, we pick up at step 6 on page 112 This is the point where the system diverges from the basic Z-haul rescue. First, lower a pulley and sling to the victim, who clips the sling to his harness (step 7a). Topside, Curly then can haul by leaning or walking backward against the rope (step 7b).

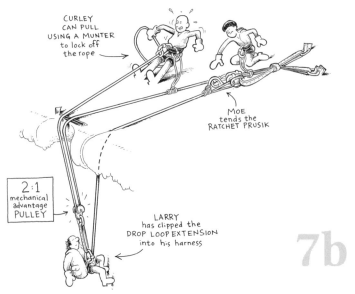

CURLEY CAN PULL USING A MUNTER to lock off the rope

MOE tends the RATCHET PRUSIK

2:1 mechanical advantage PULLEY

LARRY has clipped the DROP LOOP EXTENSION into his harness

7b

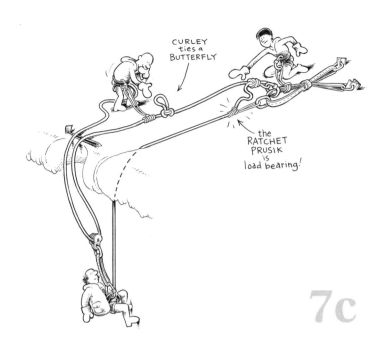

CURLEY
ties a
BUTTERFLY

the
RATCHET
PRUSIK
is
load bearing!

7c

If, after constructing the C drop, you discover it doesn't have enough mechanical advantage, you can add more mechanical advantage to the system. As also illustrated on page 129, you get a 6:1 system (steps 7c, 7d).

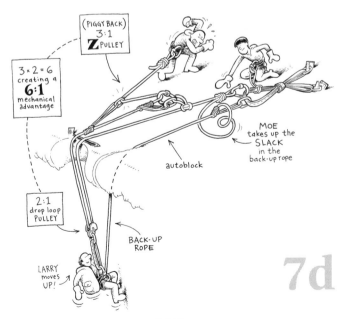

(PIGGY BACK)
3:1
Z PULLEY

3 x 2 = 6
creating a
6:1
mechanical
advantage

MOE
takes up the
SLACK
in the
back-up rope

autoblock

2:1
drop loop
PULLEY

BACK-UP
ROPE

LARRY
moves
UP!

7d

Problems to consider

Arresting the fall can be brutal if the snow surface is steep and hard. Stay alert to the conditions and terrain.

Building a solid anchor can be tough in some snow conditions. Take the time to make it bomber. Something has already gone wrong with someone in a hole, so don't skimp on the anchor. You may occasionally slam in a quick, not-so-bomber piece to get the victim's weight off of yourself or your partner, but never use this piece alone. Back it up immediately with bomber pro.

Make contact with the victim as soon as possible. Snow absorbs sound, making it almost impossible to hear each other, but if the victim is moving around,

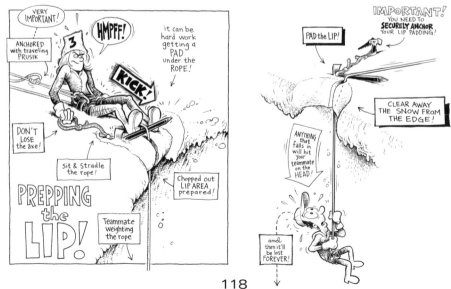

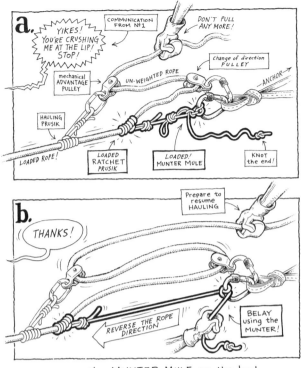

using the MUNTER MULE on the load
as a TENSION RELEASE system

you can usually feel him on the rope. If you suspect your partner is seriously hurt, you need to scramble to the lip, peer in, and see what is going on.

The lip of the crevasse can be a major problem and will factor greatly into what type of rescue you use. Taking time to properly prepare the lip is key. You must avoid hauling your partner into the lip, where he could be further injured or even killed.

CAREFUL!
Don't crush anyone
trying to haul 'em past
the lip of a crevasse!

The pack is a problem

If the victim is uninjured and is not in danger of getting hypothermic, consider getting his pack out first (step 6 in the three-person rescue.) Of course, if the victim is injured or otherwise in distress, getting him out should be the first priority.

Even if the pack doesn't seem like much of a problem, getting it out first almost always speeds things up in the end. Here are two quick methods:

1. Drop a long piece of webbing or the end of the rope, with a knot and carabiner on the end. Have the victim clip in the pack, then "hand haul" it out. This technique works great when you don't have far to haul and the pack isn't too heavy.

2. Drop a bight of rope and have the victim clip the pack onto the loop of rope. The rescuer then hauls on one side using it as a 2:1 pulley. This makes an 80-pound pack feel more like 40 pounds. Attaching a pulley as illustrated will make hauling the pack even easier.

If the victim is prusiking up the original rope, he can help guide the pack and/or direct it around the lip of the crevasse or other obstacles.

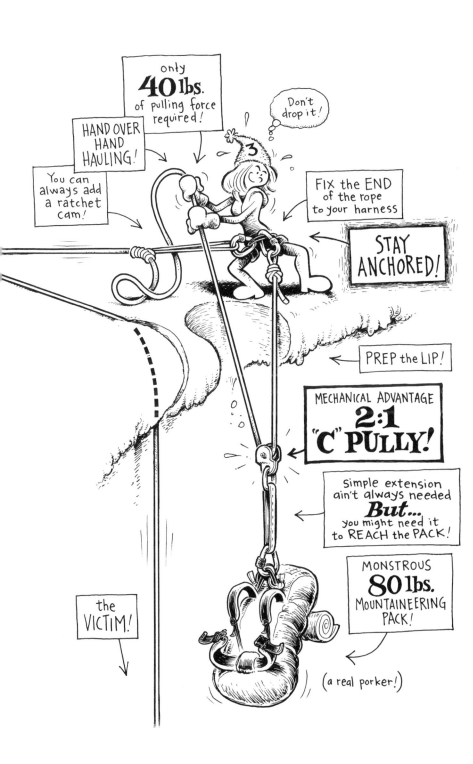

121

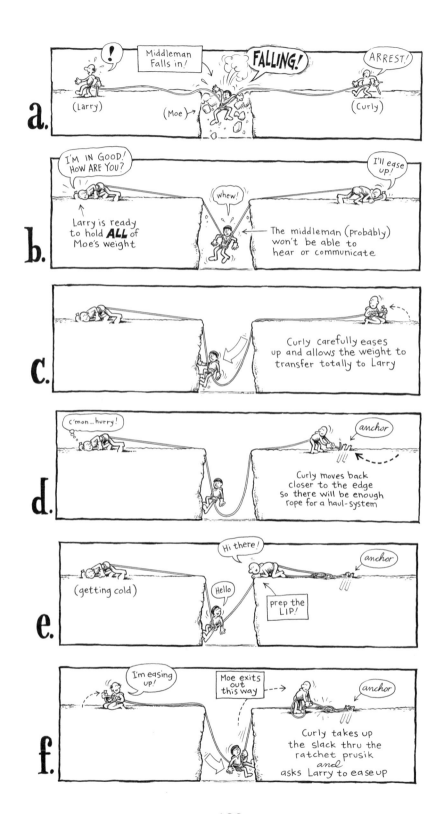

only
40 lbs.
of pulling force required!
Don't drop it!
HAND OVER HAND HAULING!
You can always add a ratchet cam!
3
FIX the END of the rope to your harness
STAY ANCHORED!
PREP the LIP!
MECHANICAL ADVANTAGE
2:1
"C" PULLY!
Simple extension ain't always needed
But...
you might need it to REACH the PACK!
MONSTROUS
80 lbs.
MOUNTAINEERING PACK!
(a real porker!)
the VICTIM!

Ratchet prusik gets sucked into the carabiner.
This is mostly a problem when only one person is topside, and has difficulty hauling and keeping the ratchet prusik properly positioned on the rope. Even if two people are available to help on top, setting the ratchet prusik so it tends itself will free up a person to help with the actual hauling. You can avoid tending the prusik and having it get sucked into the carabiner by:

1. Employing a pulley especially designed to tend the ratchet prusik (page 30). Take the time to find a light, strong, and effective one for your rope and prusik combination.

2. Using the belay-device method illustrated (right). In this scenario the belay device will act as a spacer, preventing the ratcheting prusik from being sucked into the carabiner. Note, not all belay devices will function well in this arrangement. Make sure your system combination will work.

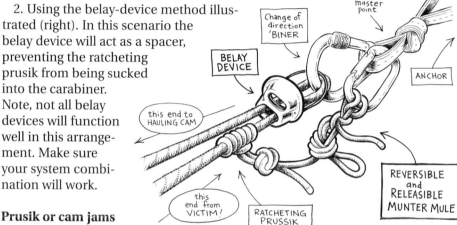

master point

Change of direction 'BINER

BELAY DEVICE

ANCHOR

this end to HAULING CAM

this end from VICTIM!

RATCHETING PRUSSIK

REVERSIBLE and RELEASIBLE MUNTER MULE

Prusik or cam jams with ice or snow.
This common problem, which can cause the prusik or cam to slip or not release, is unavoidable. All you can do is set your haul near the prusiks or cams and clear them as necessary.

An option to the Munter/Mule ratcheting prusik is the Autoblock (page 24). This is a good alternative because it can be released under tension. The Autoblock is a temperamental hitch. Make sure to test your system first, if the rope diameters don't jive it just doesn't hold. You'll need a thin cordelette and a thick rope for best results. If you have to reverse the rope direction and lower the victim, you can gently grip the coils of the Autoblock and slide them a little. The rope will release dynamically. CAUTION: back up the system before doing this!

Middle person falls in
In this event, the system will end up being similar to the one you'd construct if someone on the rope end fell in. Follow the sequence illustrated on [p. 122]. Once the fall is caught, build an anchor and tie off the rope, freeing the rescuers to move about. Eventually, all climbers on the surface will need to be by the anchors on the same side of the crevasse. Once the victim is out, the person on the side of the crevasse opposite the anchors might jump over, belayed to the rescue anchor. Or the team might echelon along the crevasse, until the victim can step or jump across at a narrower section.

1. ARREST THE FALL!

Two-person rescue

When two people are on a rope and one falls in a crevasse, the person left on the surface faces a difficult situation. She must hold a self-arrest, *and* build an anchor. If the snow is soft and anchor construction is difficult to impossible by one person, the victim — let's call her Shirley — would ideally prusik or climb out, and the person on top — Laverne — would simply hold the self-arrest and serve as the anchor.

If the snow is good, Laverne should be able to maintain the arrest with her feet, lift her upper body, remove her pack, and place a piece of protection.

Once the pro is set, Laverne can quickly attach to it by clipping her foot-loop or waist loop prusik to the anchor. She then eases back and allows Shirley's weight to transfer onto the anchor.

That was the crux. Now Laverne is free to place another piece of pro for an anchor, and then rig a Z or C-drop haul, using a self-tending ratchet prusik. If her first piece is solid, she may first want to check on Shirley. But before she does that she should back up her holding prusik by tying the rope off to the anchor.

2. BURY A PIECE OF PRO, This'll be really hard with a weighted rope!

OY!

GET OUT OF YOUR PACK — if you can!

3. CLIP the ROPE to the PRO using the FOOT PRUSIK!

Now you'll have a little freedom to build a real anchor!

Leader on white team's rope communicates with the fallen climber...

Group team rescue

Traveling with multiple rope teams has its advantages. With so many bodies and brains, trail-breaking and route-finding duties can be split up and rescues can be surprisingly easy. Large groups do, however, pose problems: it's possible to be lulled into a false sense of security, and more people can mean more confusion during a rescue. Before you head out, designate a competent rescue leader and obey him or her in emergencies.

Two rope teams make hauling out a victim easy. As the illustrations show, the leader of the "white" team moves up next to the "black" rope team, which has a team member in a crevasse (fig. a). She then prusiks her team forward, creating a bight of slack. She stays on belay using her prusiks. Next, the rest of her team attaches their prusiks (or cams) on to the black team's rope. Now, there are four people in position to haul. The white leader preps the crevasse lip, and makes sure everyone can hear (fig. b). When everything is ready, she gives the command to "HAUL," and watches the progress of the victim. To make sure everyone can hear and understands the commands, white leader should yell "STOP" shortly after the first haul command. Then continue with another haul command. Clear communication during a team haul is critical because the large forces created can easily injure the victim if he gets pinned against the crevasse wall or lip.

As the victim gets lifted (fig. c), the white leader will need to tend her prusik, or she'll be dragged back.

These larger group rescues are worth practicing. They can be fast and efficient. Again, the forces can be great, so take it slow and communicate.

Four people are now on team black's rope, ready to haul...

Two teams can generate huge hauling forces — be careful!

LIFE or DEATH... rappel to get to the victim – *IMMEDIATELY!*

Rappelling to the victim

When traveling in two or more rope teams, the second team can pull up next to the arresting team and quickly find out how the victim is doing. If the victim needs help immediately (e.g., upside down and unconscious — life and death!), it's possible for the first person on the white rope to rappel into the crevasse. Check out the illustrated sequence. White #1 will need enough rope to get down to the victim, so the white team will need to move toward the edge (fig. a). White #2 quickly connects to black's line before getting into arrest position. White #3 should prusik in and start building an anchor. White #1 can then rap down to the victim (fig. b). In this situation there would be three arresters holding the two climbers in the hole while an anchor is being constructed. White #3 can monitor the situation while he finishes the anchor and connects it to the ropes.

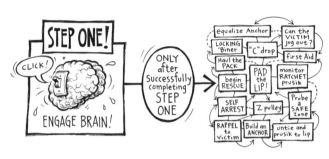

The meat of crevasse rescue, the pulley system is what you'll use to haul your incapacitated partner out of a crevasse. It is the last on the list of rescue options because of its complexity, but you must have a grip on a basic pulley set up to be proficient with crevasse rescue.

We are trying to keep this simple, leaving extraneous info out of these explanations. So things like rope stretch and friction are only mentioned. If you're a smarty-pants scientist, don't cringe too much, and if you are challenged by numbers, dive in, it won't bite!

1:1 haul

Hauling systems can be as basic as the 1:1 (read "one to one") pulley and ascender you use for dragging bags up a big wall. The 1:1 system works for wall climbing, but since it requires 100 pounds of pulling force to lift 100 pounds of weight, it's application is limited on a glacier where your partner and gear can easily weight 200 pounds. Add to this the friction caused by the rope cutting into the snow, and the more mechanically advantageous 2:1 and 3:1 systems may be necessary. Note that in a 1:1 system the load raises one foot for every foot you haul in, and, more importantly, the load on the anchor is double that of the load you haul.

Then again the simple and fast-to-build 1:1 may be just what you need. Three or more people hauling on a 1:1 system might generate enough lift to raise their comrade out of the crevasse.

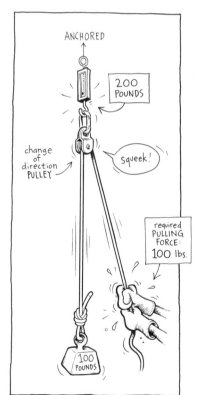

1:1 PULLEY SYSTEM

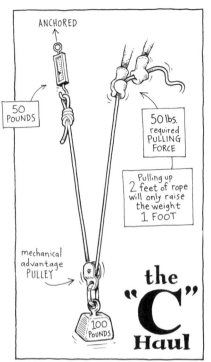

ANCHORED

50
POUNDS

50 lbs.
required
PULLING
FORCE

Pulling up
2 feet of rope
will only raise
the weight
1 FOOT

mechanical
advantage
PULLEY

the "C" Haul

2:1 PULLEY SYSTEM

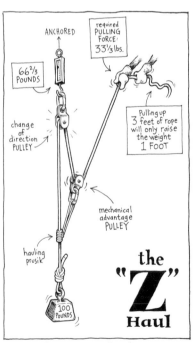

ANCHORED

required
PULLING
FORCE:
33⅓ lbs.

66⅔
POUNDS

change
of
direction
PULLEY

Pulling up
3 feet of rope
will only raise
the weight
1 FOOT

mechanical
advantage
PULLEY

hauling
prusik

100
POUNDS

the "Z" Haul

3:1 PULLEY SYSTEM

2:1 haul

When you don't have the people to put a 1:1 to good use, you might use the 2:1 "C" haul system, which lifts 100 pounds for every 50 pounds of pulling force. The 2:1 is simply the 1:1 with the pulley attached to the load instead of the anchor. Disadvantages: the 2:1 only raises the load one foot for every two feet of rope you haul in, and you can only haul half the length of the rope. It is also harder to set up since you need to get a bite of rope to your partner in the crevasse.

3:1 haul

For crevasse rescue, the 3:1 "Z" haul system is often easier to set up than the 2:1, and lifts three pounds for every pound you haul on the rope. The 2:1 C and the 3:1 Z systems are the two you need to learn. In most cases either of these two systems will suffice for crevasse extraction.

Stacked hauls

When you need even more mechanical advantage, you can piggy back one system on another and multiply the advantage. Stack a 2:1 on another 2:1 you get a 4:1. Stack a 2:1 on a 3:1 and you get a 6:1. Stack a 3:1 on a 3:1 and you have the powerful 9:1. Caution to the rescuer: If you need to resort to these stacked systems there might be something else going on that is creating a problem. Check your system set up before adding advantage.

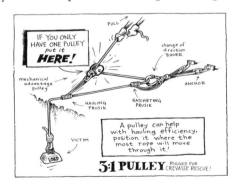

PULL

IF YOU ONLY
HAVE ONE PULLEY
put it
HERE!

change of
direction
BINER

mechanical
advantage
pulley

ANCHOR

HAULING
PRUSIK

RATCHETING
PRUSIK

VICTIM

A pulley can help
with hauling efficiency,
position it where the
most rope will move
through it!

LOAD

3:1 PULLEY RIGGED FOR CREVASSE RESCUE!

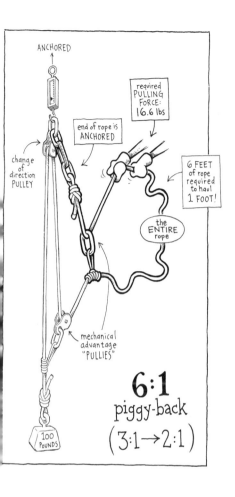

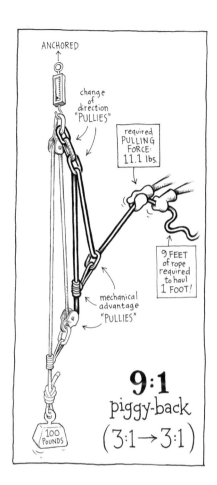

Rope friction

With all systems, the drag of the rope through pulleys and carabiners will reduce the mechanical advantage. Pulleys have less drag than carabiners, but even good ones are only 83 percent efficient; this adds 17 pounds to every 100 pounds you try to lift (takes 117 pounds of force to lift a 100-pound load). Carabiners are even less efficient: a single oval is but 70 percent efficient; doubled ovals are 68-percent efficient. The moral? Build simple but efficient systems.

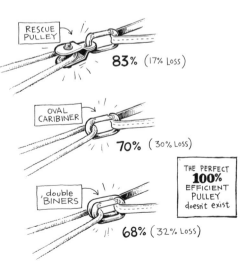

(serious!)

As climbers, it is our responsibility to take care of ourselves. Rescuers have died performing rescues, which consume large amounts of time and resources. Nature-loving visitors would be appalled at the tremendous impact a rescue has on the environment: Areas are chain sawed clear for landing sites, waste is left in the wilderness, there's all the fuel consumed by the various machines, and the lives of rescuers put at risk.

Mountaineering is risky, though it is only recreation. If we choose risky play we should accept its consequences. Yet some people refuse to accept responsibility for themselves and venture out unprepared. Witness the frequency of helicopter rescues in Europe and many parts of North America.

We aren't arguing against life-saving rescues, but suggest that many rescues would be unnecessary if everyone knew how to safely travel on a glacier, and was prepared to self-rescue if something went wrong. A helicopter rescue is not the hand of God; it is a large group of dedicated people and resources undertaking a dangerous mission. Before you head into the mountains ask yourself, "What will we do if something bad happens?" If you expect or require someone else's help, stay home.

The bizarre reality of solo-glacier-travel

General mountaineering

Accidents in North American Mountaineering, Williamson, Powter editors, The American Alpine Club, annual.

Alpine Climbing, John Barry, The Crowood Press,1988.

Climbing Ice, Yvon Chouinard, Sierra Club, 1978.

Glaciers, Michael Strong, Falcon Press.

Glacier Travel and Crevasse Rescue, second edition, Andy Selters, The Mountaineers, 1999.

Ice: Tools and Technique, Duane Raleigh, Climbing Magazine (illustrated by Mike Clelland) 1995.

Mountaineering: The Freedom of the Hills, sixth edition, Graydon and Hanson Editors, The Mountaineers,1997.

Getting **OUT** of your pack needs to be easy!

put things lik CAMERAS and GEAR SLINGS **UNDER** your back pac

Gently LOWER your pack so you don't shock load the anchor!

re-enforced haul loop

ice axe leash, GOOD!

(easily removed & dropped)

carry coils **OVER** your back pac so the rope is accessible

When dropping the pack **always** undo your hip belt **first**, then undo shoulder straps

au cheval

NOLS Wilderness Mountaineering, Phil Powers, Stackpole, 1993.
Rock: Tools and Technique, Michael Benge and Duane Raleigh, Climbing Magazine, 1995.
Surviving Denali, Jonathan Waterman, American Alpine Club Press, 1983.

Knots, slings, and technical things
Climbing Anchors, John Long, Chockstone Press, 1993.
Knots and Ropes for Climbers, Duane Raleigh (illustrations by Mike Clelland), Stackpole Books, 1998.
Self Rescue, David Fasulo (illustrations by Mike Clelland), Falcon Publishing.

Winter, skiing, and avalanche skills
Allen & Mikes' Really Cool Backcountry Ski Book, Allen O'Bannon, with illustrations by Mike Clelland, Falcon Publishing, 1996.
Free Heel Skiing, second edition, Paul Parker, The Mountaineers, 1995.
Ski Mountaineering, Peter Cliff, Pacific Search Press Seattle, 1987.
Snow Sense, Fredston and Fesler, Alaska Mountain Safety Center Inc., 1994.

First Aid
Medicine for Mountaineering, The Mountaineers.
Going Higher, Charles Houston, M.D., Little, Brown and Company, third edition 1987.
NOLS Wilderness First Aid, Shimilfinig and Lindsey.

Weather and general information

Eric Sloane's Weather Book, Erik Sloan, Hawthorn Books, 1952.

Glaciers, Sharp, University of Oregon Books, 1960.

Glacier Ice, LaChapelle, The Mountaineers, 1971.

Glaciers of North America, Sue Ferguson, Fulcrum Publishing, 1992.

Northwest Mountain Weather, Jeff Renner, The Mountaineers, 1992.

The Weather Book, Jack Williams, USA Today, Vintage Books, 1992.

Winter, An Ecological Handbook, Halfpenny, Ozanne, and Biesiot, Johnson Publishing Company, 1989.

Tin Tin in Tibet, Hergé, Little, and Brown, Boston, 1960.

Guidebooks

Cascade Alpine Guide, Vol. I, II, and III, Fred Becky, The Mountaineers.

Denali Climbing Guide, R.J. Secor (illustrations by Mike Clelland), Stackpole Books, 1998.

Alaska: A Climbing Guide, Colby Coombs, Mike Wood, The Mountaineers, 2002

Denali's West Buttress, Colby Coombs, The Mountaineers, 1997.

High Alaska, Jonathan Waterman, AAC Press, 1988.

Magazines and outdoor education

Alpine Ascents International, Seattle Washington, www.alpineascents.com

Climbing Magazine, www.climbing.com

National Outdoor Leadership School (NOLS), www.nols.edu

Creative Energies, www.creativeenergies.biz

Authors

Andy Tyson grew up climbing trees in the hills of Pennsylvania. He started his rock-climbing career in Ohio, where he also studied geology. Soon after his graduation he moved to the western mountains. Andy spent 10 years working for the National Outdoor Leadership School (NOLS). He also works for Alpine ascents International where he enjoys guiding the world's high peaks as well as training aspiring climbers and guides. He is part owner of Creative Energies, a renewable energy company based in Wyoming. Andy has enjoyed climbing in many mountain ranges including the central Rockies, North Cascades, Canadian Coast Range, Alaska ranges, the Andies of southern Chile, Ellsworth Range in Antarctica, and the Himalaya. He now makes his home in Seattle.

Mike Clelland never went to art school, studying *Mad Magazine* instead. He grew up in the flat plains of Michigan, then spent 10 years (as a Yuppie!) in New York City. In 1987 he, thought it might be fun to be a ski bum in Wyoming for the winter. Unfortunately, after living and skiing in the Rockies, he found it impossible to return to the Big Apple. Mike lives in a shed in Idaho which houses his international world headquarters, as well as his cats. He divides his time illustrating and instructing for NOLS. Mike is a frequent contributor to *Climbing*.

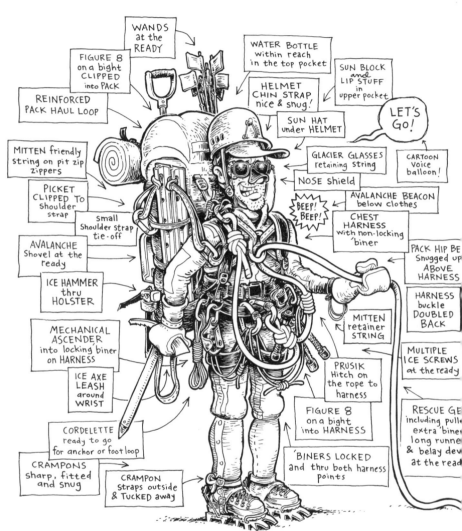

it's bliss on the glacier!